黔中遗珍

贵安新区出土文物精粹

贵州省文物考古研究所
中国社会科学院考古研究所
贵州省博物馆
四川大学历史文化学院
成都文物考古研究所
贵安新区党工委管委会

编

科学出版社
北京

内 容 简 介

　　本书是首部全面介绍贵安新区可移动文物的公开出版物，以收录贵安新区出土清代及以前学术性较强、观赏性较强的文物为主，按照动物化石、石器、骨角器、陶瓷器、金银器、铜铁器、服饰七个部分进行分类，以图为主，图文并茂，进行了比较全面的梳理和研究，全面反映了贵安新区出土文物的概貌、重点、特点和价值，具有较高的学术性、资料性和科普性。

图书在版编目(CIP)数据

黔中遗珍:贵安新区出土文物精粹 / 贵州省文物考古研究所等编. —北京: 科学出版社, 2016.9

ISBN 978-7-03-049921-9

Ⅰ.①黔… Ⅱ.①贵… Ⅲ.①出土文物－贵州－图集 Ⅳ.①K873.732

中国版本图书馆CIP数据核字 (2016) 第220583号

责任编辑: 柴丽丽／责任校对: 邹慧卿
责任印制: 肖　兴／书籍设计: 北京美光设计制版有限公司

科 学 出 版 社 出版

北京东黄城根北街16号
邮政编码: 100717
http://www.sciencep.com

文物出版社印刷厂 印刷

科学出版社发行　各地新华书店经销

*

2016年9月第 一 版　　开本: 889×1194　1/16
2016年9月第一次印刷　　印张: 13
字数: 374 000

定价: 238.00元

守望乡愁　传承文脉

　　人民是国家文明的创造者，是泽被后世的民族文脉的守护者，同样人民也是历史的书写者和传承者。千秋煌煌，万载悠悠，中华文明恢弘壮丽，当我们翻开这篇波澜壮阔的历史巨制，我们祖先创造出的灿烂文化闪耀在我们的眼前，让我们感受到了无比的自豪和耀目的光芒。

　　古往今来，朝代更替兴衰，多少帝王将相灰飞烟灭，化成一捧黄土随风飘去，其实肉体逝去是天道规律，唯独不死的是千百年来我们的祖先开疆拓土和缔造文明的精神，以及他们留存下来的亘古不灭的文化遗产。

　　十八大以来，习近平总书记十分关心中国的文物事业，到地方考察调研十分关心文物保护工作，并多次就文物保护工作作出重要批示。2014年2月25日，他在北京考察时强调，"历史文化是城市的灵魂，要像爱惜自己的生命一样保护好城市历史文化遗产"；2016年4月12日全国文物工作会议，总书记对文物工作作出重要指示，他强调，"文物承载灿烂文明，传承历史文化，维系民族精神，是老祖宗留给我们的宝贵遗产，是加强社会主义精神文明建设的深厚滋养。保护文物功在当代、利在千秋"。

　　近年来，我省考古工作取得了一系列重要成果，引起了海内外的瞩目。遵义海龙囤遗址成功入选世界文化遗产名录，遵义杨价墓等一大批重要遗存先后荣获多项国家和国际荣誉。唐代诗人李白曾有诗云："杨花落尽子规啼，闻道龙标过五溪。我寄愁心与明月，随风直到夜郎西。"一直以来，这寄托了李大诗人愁心的夜郎之地——贵州，一直被贴着闭塞、落后的标签。今天，人们万万没有想到，贵州这个"夜郎之地"，竟然孕育着丰富多彩且悠久深厚的历史文化。

　　以贵安新区为中心的黔中地区，从新中国成立至今，陆续有重大考古发现，从数万年前开始，每个历史时段都有时代识别性很好的代表性遗存发现，如平坝飞虎山洞穴遗址、马场牛坡洞遗址、高峰招果洞遗址和马场魏晋南北朝墓葬群等，均填补了贵州史前时期和魏晋南北朝时期的很多空白，是贵州境内目前建立起从史前到明清时期完整考古文化序列的唯一地区。

自贵安新区开发建设以来，就很重视对新区区域内历史文化的挖掘、研究和保护，本着对历史文物的敬畏之心，树立起保护文物也是政绩的科学理念，统筹努力做好文物保护与经济社会发展工作，全面贯彻落实中央提出的"保护为主、抢救第一、合理利用、加强管理"的工作方针。通过建区以来这几年田野考古调查和发掘工作的持续系统推进，取得了一系列重大成果，逐渐清晰了对贵安历史文化面貌的认知。

通过核查，仅在新区马场、高峰境内就发现各类文化遗产81项（含地下文物50处、地面文物27处、非物质文化遗产4项）。其中地下文物包括史前至商周时期的洞穴遗址38处、两汉魏晋南北朝至唐代的墓葬和遗址4处、唐宋至明清时期的遗址和墓葬7处、近现代墓葬1处；地面文物包括洞屯及营盘遗址9处、寺庙2处、村落文化景观7处、古井古桥古塔及碑刻9处；非物质文化遗产包括苗族夫妻舞、布依族六月六等4项。

通过开展多方合作，贵州省文物考古研究所联合中国社会科学院考古研究所、四川大学历史文化学院、成都文物考古研究所等科研单位和高校，对史前洞穴遗址马场牛坡洞、高峰招果洞和汉晋墓葬群等文物点进行了调查和考古发掘，取得了重大收获，已经出土石器、骨器、动物化石等各类文物数千件。从目前考古工作得出的信息，古人类在马场牛坡洞生活的历史上溯到距今1万多年到距今3000多年前；在高峰招果洞遗址生活历史更加久远，上溯到距今3万~2万年到距今5000~4000年。这两处洞穴遗址文化堆积层厚重，序列完整，且发展持续，在全国考古史上十分难得。以牛坡洞遗址和招果洞遗址为代表的洞穴遗址群考古发掘，对解决西南地区陶器起源、农业起源、家畜畜养起源等一系列重大学术问题研究意义重大，下一步的工作十分值得期待。

发挥独特的地域文化旅游资源的优势，激发魅力厚重的文物资源，是我们贵安一个重要的功能定位，这一科学定位决定了生态保护和文化建设是城市规划和城市建设的生命线。贵安新区自然风光绮丽，除部分少数民族文化外，似乎缺少更深层次的文化支撑，考古发掘不断浮出土面的文物，蕴藏了丰富的历史文化信息，恰如其分地填补了这一缺憾，是以后贵安新区宝贵的文化旅游和人文资源，将来甚至会成为贵安新区的城市文化名片。现在考古工作虽刚刚起步，重要发现和成果却已初露端倪，随着考古工作的深入开展，贵安新区蕴藏已久的神秘历史面纱，将会被缓缓揭开。

秦如培常务副省长高度重视文物保护工作，亲自指示在马场镇熊家坡墓地选址建设贵州省文物考古研究所贵安整理基地和贵州省公共考古活动中心，目前已经完成征地工作，即将进入施工阶段，该中心建成后将成为贵州首个系统地向公众展示历史文化、普及考古知识的科普平台，同时作为考古成果的科研转化中心，配备先进的文物保护、检测分析设备仪器。届时，公共考古中心将免费对普通民众开放，人们可以真正参与到田野考古发掘和科研工作中来，真正让考古走出象牙塔，成为普通民众文化餐桌上的一道美味佳肴。

因为喀斯特地貌，贵州史前洞穴遗址广布于贵州地区，对于研究人类从旧石器时代往新石器时代过渡时期的文化历史以及从狩猎到农耕文明的转型研究均有着重要意义，这在中国乃至世界范围内，都有着典型性和代表性，从洞穴遗址的密布和文化的延续看，甚至是唯一性的！而贵安新区境内河网密布，生态良好，天然喀斯特洞穴发育，是目前贵州境内洞穴遗址分布最为集中的地区，是远古人类栖息的美好家园，古人类在此繁衍生息数万年，留下了丰富的遗迹、遗物。为利用好这一得天独厚的资源，我们将依托贵安新区境内的洞穴遗址，深入开展国内国际学术合作，建设"中国南方喀斯特洞穴遗址公园"项目，休闲之余，成为窥见原始人类生活场景的一扇窗口，也将成为贵安新区文化建设一道亮丽的风景线。

贵安新区在今后的考古发掘和研究进程中，还有很多工作需要落实，文物考古单位、新区各有关部门（单位）要发扬好省委陈敏尔书记 2016 年 3 月 22 日在遵义海龙囤遗址调研时对省考古研究所提出的"孜孜不倦、甘于清贫、甘于寂寞"的考古精神，严格遵从严谨的科学人文精神，把祖先赐予我们贵安这块充满新生活力的厚厚的历史积淀完美地呈现出来，并使之发挥出巨大的社会价值作用。我们更应着眼未来，高瞻远瞩，积极传承和保护这些宝贵的"乡愁历史文化"，继往开来，为天地立正心，为国家长精神，为民族守文脉，为中华文化的伟大复兴继绝学、开太平。

马长青

PREFACE

Basing on the Native Culture, Inheriting the Cultural Context

The people are creators of national civilization, guardians of the national cultural context which will benefit our posterity, and writers and inheritors of the history. With the thousands of year's history, Chinese civilization is so magnificent; when we opened the spectacular history, the splendid culture that our ancestors created was sparkling before our eyes, let us feel very proud in the dazzling ray of light.

Through the ages, dynasties alternated, how many kings and emperors gone with the wind; actually death is the natural law, but our ancestors' spirit of exploiting the boundary and creating the civilization will never die; the eternal cultural heritage they left for us will never die.

Since the 18th CPC national congress, the General Secretary Xi Jinping deeply concerned about China's cultural relics, he also very concerned about the protection of cultural relics when he was in the local investigation research work. He has made several important instructions on the protection of cultural relics. On February 25, 2014, when he was on a visit to Beijing, he stressed that "history culture is the soul of the city, we should protect city historical and cultural heritage just like cherish our own lives"; on April 12, 2016, on the national work conference on cultural relics, he made important instructions of the work of cultural relics, he stressed that "cultural relics bear splendid civilization, inherit history and culture, maintain the national spirit; it is the priceless heritage the ancestors left for us; it will strengthen the construction of socialist spiritual civilization; cultural relics protection is a mission done at present, but it will benefit the future generation."

In recent years, the archaeological work in Guizhou province has made a series of important achievements, has attracted attention from home and abroad. Hailongtun site of Zunyi was successfully inscribed on the world cultural heritage list, Yangjia tomb of Zunyi and a large number of other important heritages had won many national and international honors. Tang Dynasty poet Li Bai had written a poem, "flowers fall, cuckoos chirp; I heard of that you have been demoted far away; I was so worried about you; my prayer will accompany with you till the west of Yelang." Yelang was the old name of Guizhou; for a long time, this place was always been labeled as out-of-the-way and backward. Today, we never thought that, a rich, colorful, long and profound historical culture was generated unexpectedly in such a place.

Since the establishment of the People's Republic of China, there were many important archaeological discoveries in central Guizhou, especially in Guian New District. Tens of thousands of years ago, representative heritages with distinct chronicle identification have been found in every historical period, such as Feihushan cave site in Pingba, Niupodong site in Machang, Zhaoguodong site in Gaofeng, and Machang cemetery of Wei, Jin, Northern and Southern Dynasties. These sites filled much blank of prehistoric times and Wei, Jin, Northern and Southern Dynasties in Guizhou. This area is the only one which can establish a complete archaeological culture sequence from the prehistoric times to Ming and Qing Dynasties in present Guizhou.

Since Guian New District has been developed and constructed, we took much count of exploration, research and protection on the history and culture in this district. With the respect of historical relics, we set up the scientific concept, i.e. "protection of cultural relics is a kind of political achievements", and we took efforts to do a good job of cultural relics protection and economic and social development as a whole, comprehensively implement the work guidelines—"protection is given priority; salvage on the first; rational utilization; management strengthened." Through the years of field archaeological investigation and excavation continuously and systematically since this district has been found, we gained a series of significant achievements, and we also gradually make clear the cognition to historical and cultural features of Guian.

Through the verification, there are 81 sites of various kinds of cultural heritage found in Machang and Gaochang (50 sites of underground cultural relics, 27 sites of ground cultural relics, and 4 items of intangible cultural heritage). The underground cultural relics include 38 sites of prehistoric cave sites of Shang and Zhou Dynasties, 4 cemeteries and sites of Western and Eastern Han Dynasties, Wei, Jin, Northern and Southern Dynasties, and Tang Dynasty, 7 sites and cemeteries of Tang, Song, Ming, Qing Dynasties, and a modern cemetery. The ground cultural relics include 9 sites of *dongtun* (the wall in front of a cave for defense) and *yingpan* (the wall on the top of a mountain for defense), 2 sites of temples, 7 sites of village cultural landscape, 9 sites of ancient wells, bridges, towers and inscriptions. The intangible cultural heritages include the "couple dance" of Miao nationality, the festival at "6th of June" of Buyi nationality, and other 2 items.

Through multilateral cooperation, Guizhou Provincial Institute of Cultural Relics and Archaeology combined with the Institute of Archaeology of Chinese Academy of Social Sciences, The History and Culture Institute of Sichuan University, Chengdu Municipal Institute of Cultural Relics and Archaeology and other scientific research units, colleges and universities, carried out investigation and archaeological excavation on prehistoric cave sites (Niupodong in Machang, Zhaoguodong in Gaofeng) and cemeteries of Han and Jin Dynasties, and made significant gains—thousands of cultural relics unearthed, including stone and bone artifacts, animal fossils and others. According to the information of current archaeological work, 10000 years ago to about 3000 years ago, ancient human had lived at Niupodong in Machang; they lived at Zhaoguodong in Gaofeng for a even much longer time (30000−20000 years ago to 5000−4000 years ago).

The culture accumulation of these two cave sites are thick and various, and the sequence is complete and the culture developed continuously, which is very rare in Chinese archaeological history. These archaeological excavations on cave sites (taking Niupodong site and Zhaoguodong site as representatives) is of great significance to solve a series of important academic problems of the research, such as the origin of pottery, of agriculture, of livestock farming in the southwest area; the work in the future should be worthy to expect fully.

Playing the advantages of the unique regional culture tourism resources and stimulating the charm of cultural relic resources, this is the important function of Guian which determines that, the ecological and cultural construction is the lifeline of urban planning and urban construction. Guian New District has beautiful natural scenery, but in addition to the part of minority culture, it seems to be lack of deeper cultural support; cultural relics which contain a wealth of historical and cultural information constantly unearthed from archaeological excavations, properly fill this blank; they will be precious cultural tourism and cultural resources of Guian New District, even will become the city's cultural card of Guian New District in the future. Archaeological work is just beginning now, key findings and results have made first appearance, with the in-depth development of archaeological work, and the mysterious veil of the long history of Guian New District will be uncovered slowly.

Guizhou executive vice governor, Mr. Qin Rupei, attaches great importance to the work for the protection of cultural relics, and personally instructed to set up the Guian Base of Guizhou Provincial Institute of Archaeology and Cultural Relics and Guizhou Provincial Public Archaeological Activity Center at Xiongjiapo cemetery of Machang. Now the land requisition work has been completed, the construction will be the next step. After the completion of the center, it will be the first science platform in Guizhou to show the public the history and culture, to popularize the knowledge of archaeology systematically; at the same time, as the archaeological achievements of scientific research center, it will be equipped with advanced detection equipment and instruments for the protection of cultural relics. Then the public archaeological center will be open free to common people, all of us can really involved in the field excavation and research work, making archaeology out of the ivory tower actually and become a cultural enjoyment for ordinary people.

Because of the karst topography, prehistoric cave sites distributed all over Guizhou, which has important significance for the research on human cultural history of the transition from the Paleolithic Age to the Neolithic Age, and for the research on the transition from the hunting civilization to the farming civilization. These cave sites are typical and representative in China and even all over the world, from the point of the dense distribution and continuation of culture, they are rather unique. Guian New

District is covered densely by river network, therefore the ecology here is rather fine, and natural karst caves develop well; there are most cave sites distributed in this district. Here is the homeland of ancient people, they lived here for tens of thousands of years, leaving abundant cultural heritage. To make good use of the advantageous resources, relying on these cave sites in Guian New District, we will deeply carry on domestic and international academic cooperation, and carry on the construction project of "Karst Cave Site Park in South China"; we hope that this park could become a window from which we can take a glimpse on the original human life scenes, and a beautiful scenery of the culture construction in Guian New District.

In the process of excavation and research in Guian New District, there will be much more work to do in the future, units of cultural reiics and archaeology, departments (and units) of Guian New District should develop the spirit of archaeology which was raised by Guizhou provincial party committee secretary, Mr. Chen Min'er on March 22, 2016, when he took investigation and survey with Guizhou Provincial Institute of Archaeology and Cultural Relics—"working tirelessly; willing to be poor; willing to be lonely". We will strictly comply with the rigorous scientific humanistic spirit, and show up the thick historical accumulation full of new vitality which ancestors gave us, and make it play a role of a great social value. Furthermore, we should focus on the future, take a broad and long-term view, and actively inherit and protect the valuable "homesickness culture and history," for the country's spirit, for the national cultural context, for the great rejuvenation of the Chinese culture, we will inherit ancestors' wisdom, and initiate another great millennium.

Ma Changqing

2014 年 1 月 6 日，国务院批复设立贵州贵安新区，为中国第八个国家级新区，被赋予建设西部地区重要经济增长极、内陆开放型经济新高地、生态文明示范区三大战略定位，贵安新区包括贵阳市和安顺市的 21 个乡镇（街道办），312 个行政村，总面积 1795 平方公里，现状人口 79 万。贵安新区所处的黔中丘原盆地区地处贵州高原的第二个阶梯面上，海拔在 1000~1500 米，这一区域地貌总体特点是河谷较宽浅，地势较平缓，丘陵起伏，坝子连片。该区内分布最广的地貌类型是岩溶丘陵和开阔的溶蚀盆地以及峰林盆地等。属于亚热带湿润型季风气候，年均气温 18.3℃，1 月平均气温 6℃，极端最低温度 -7.4℃。7 月平均气温 23.5℃，属亚热带湿润型季风气候。境内河流纵横，主要河流有三岔河、老营河、乐平河、羊昌河等，属长江水系。基本地貌形态开始形成于新生代喜马拉雅造山运动之后的山盆期。优越的自然环境，孕育了悠久的历史文化，目前已探明至少在旧石器时代晚期就有人类在此生息繁衍，留下了丰富的文化遗产。

一、贵安考古回顾及主要收获

贵安新区境内的考古工作始于 1954 年，距今已经走过了 60 余年的历程。

1954 年，在羊昌河水利工程建设中发现了汉代文物，当时的省博物馆考古队追踪线索，首次在贵州境内发现了汉代墓葬，证明在汉代，中央王朝已经开始在此地经营开发。1956~1959 年对原清镇、平坝交界处的汉墓群进行了四次较大规模清理。第一次于 1956 年春天，在金家大坪发掘汉墓 2 座；第二次于 1957 年春天，在平庄、老鸡场发掘墓葬 7 座；第三次从 1957 年 12 月中旬到 1958 年 2 月初，在清镇县琊珑坝、苗坟坡发掘古墓葬 19 座；第四次发掘从 1958 年 12 月至 1959 年 4 月，在清镇平坝交界处尹关、琊珑坝、芦狄哨和土门寨等地清理墓葬 140 余座。四次发掘共清理了墓葬 160 多座，年代自汉代至宋代，墓葬形制以土坑墓居多，占四分之三以上，其余为石室墓，出土大量的陶器、瓷器、漆器、铜器、金器、银器、织物等丰富的遗物。1965～1966 年，贵州省博物馆考古组在今贵安新区马场镇附近的万人坟、熊家坡、大松山等地清理了古墓葬 34 座，其中包括 16 座东晋南朝墓葬，出土了丰富的陶、瓷、漆、铜、金、银器等珍贵文物。1981 年，贵州省博物馆对平坝县白云镇飞虎山洞穴遗址进行了发掘，第一次在今贵安新区境内发现了史前洞穴遗址，碳十四测定的最老年代为距今约 13000 年，在飞虎山遗址发现了大量的石器、骨角器、陶片等，打制石制品 532 件，磨制石器 21 件，骨角器 79 件，陶片 2000 余片。

近五年来，随着贵安新区的建设步伐加快，为配合贵安新区项目建设的考古调查和抢救性考古发掘工作力度不断加大，为配合基础建设的田野考古和为解决贵州中西部史前洞穴遗址相关学术问题的主动性考古工作齐头并进，贵安新区的考古工作得到了突飞猛进的发展。

2013 年，应贵州省文化厅、文物局的安排，贵州省文物考古研究所启动了对贵安新区境内地下文物资源的普查工作，在既往工作的基础上，再一次进行了更详尽深入全面的调查。仅在直管区的马场、高峰、湖潮、党武四个乡镇就发现史前至商周时期的洞穴遗址 38 处，两汉魏晋南北朝、唐宋至明清时期的墓葬数百座，进一步摸清了贵安新区地下文物资源的蕴藏情况。

2013 年，为配合贵安新区项目建设的基本建设考古工作大规模启动，现该项工作仍在密切跟进中。据不完全统计，我所共在贵安新区境内开展基建文物调查项目约 100 个，其中交通建设项目约 60 个，园区、水库、安置点约 40 个，取得了重要收获。如磊庄至马场公路建设，通过对公路施工范围及周边地区进行了比较细致的调查勘探工作，新发现了沙坡和杨家桥两处魏晋南朝至唐代古遗址，经初步钻探证实，遗址区内存在一些早晚不同时期的古墓葬。2014 年 2～5 月，我们对沙坡遗址进行了系统发掘，并在杨家桥遗址进行了大规模的系统钻探工作，新发现魏晋南朝至宋明时期古墓葬 70 余座，并对其中的 3 座墓葬进行了清理。2014 年，为配合平坝迎宾大道建设，对夏云镇汉墓群进行了清理，共清理墓葬 5 座。出土陶、铜、铁、银、琉璃器等各类文物 20 余件。

从 2012 年 10 月至今，中国社会科学院考古研究所、贵州省文物考古研究所联合对马场镇牛坡洞遗址进行了持续 5 年的发掘，揭露面积约 90 平方米。共发现墓葬 6 座、灰坑 6 处，获得了大量地层关系明确的文化遗物，包括陶片、石器、骨器等生活用具、生产工具以及大量与加工打制石器有关的石料、断块、石核、石片、碎屑等和水、陆生动物遗骸等。2014 年 7 月，贵州省文物考古研究所、四川大学考古学系、成都文物考古研究所联合对马场镇大湾洞遗址进行了小规模试掘，此次发掘主要在洞外进行，出土石制品 105 件，还有部分哺乳动物骨骼和少量陶片。2016 年，贵州省文物考古研究所、四川大学考古学系、成都文物考古研究所对高峰镇招果洞遗址进行试掘，出土了大量的陶片、石器、骨角器、动物骨骼等文物近万件，特别集中出土大量精美的骨角器，按器形大致可分为铲和锥两类，并出土了数量可观的水生动物骨骼，如蚌、螺、鱼等，遗址反映出旧石器时代晚期至新石器时代早期黔中洞穴居民对动物资源利用达到空前的广度和深度，体现了低纬高原山地居民独特的生计方式和对山地环境独特的应对策略，从剖面看，遗址堆积巨厚，具有极大的工作潜力。

在考古工作推进的同时，为配合宣传，我们开展了系列公众考古活动。2016 年 7 月，组织贵阳市第一中学、贵州省师范大学附属中学考古社的同学，进入高峰镇招果洞遗址考古工地，参与到考古发掘中，对现场发掘、石器打制、考古钻探、植物浮选等考古工作流程进行了现场体验。受社会上流行的盗墓小说影响，同学们对考古充满了好奇，以为考古工作是惊险刺激和神秘莫测的，通过切身的感受，对考古有了更实际和直观的认识，更接触到了考古的"地气"，认识到了人类历经数万年的沧桑变迁，文化遗产能保留到现在是十分不易的，而考古对于历史碎片的挖掘和拼接，某种程度上说是琐碎、枯燥甚至相当艰苦的，要从考古的渠道实现对历史的认知，不仅仅是好奇能实现的，更需要付出艰辛的劳动。与此同时，同学们也感受到和书本历史知识的截然不同，感受到了考古的丰富、生动和趣味性，认识到了考古是一门解释人类本身从哪里来、是帮助人类找回丢失的记忆的学问，培养了同学们对考古学这一触摸历史的学科门类的兴趣。此次借中国（贵州）第二届国际民族民间工艺品文化产品博览会之机举办贵安新区考古成果展，本身就是一次很好的公众考古宣传活动，将多年来的考古成果集中汇报展示，增进广大市民对贵安新区历史文化面貌及发展轨迹的认知，让考古成果更好地发挥其社会效益，更好地为贵安新区建设服务。

二、贵安考古的特殊意义

从目前已经发现的考古资料看，贵安考古在贵州考古中具有独特性、唯一性、代表性和典型性，有着重要意义。

贵安新区的丘陵低山地带，是典型的中国南方喀斯特地貌，洞穴分布广泛，是贵州远古人类的天然栖息家园，是贵州史前洞穴遗址最为集中分布的地区，这在中国乃至世界范围内，都有着典型性和代表性，从洞穴遗址的密布和文化的延续看，甚至是唯一性的。此外，贵安新区是贵州自数万年前的旧石器时代至明清时期，考古遗存序列唯一完整的地区，是以考古学完整书写贵州通史的唯一地区。而且，在贵安新区，发现了贵州唯一的一块彩陶。可见贵安考古在贵州考古中的独特性、唯一性、代表性和典型性，对贵州乃至中国西南地区历史脉络的梳理，有着重大意义。

贵州古人类活动的历史，可以上溯到更新世中期，以盘县大洞遗址、黔西观音洞遗址、桐梓岩灰洞遗址为代表。贵安新区所处的黔中地区，河网密布，喀斯特洞穴发育，生态环境极佳，进入晚更新世以后，黔中地区人类活动逐渐频繁，从高峰镇招果洞遗址的测年数据来看，从距今3万～2万年，这一区域已经有古人类活动，择洞而居，琢石为器，磨骨成锥，刮皮结衣，我们的先祖们围坐在一堆堆篝火旁，伴随着一次次浑厚的敲击，在黎明前的子夜，叩开了人类文明之门。贵安新区的洞穴遗址对解决新旧石器时代过渡时期的诸多重大学术问题，如原始农业起源、家畜畜养、陶器起源都有重要的意义，对建立贵州史前考古学文化序列，将起到重大推动作用。

1981年，在贵安新区飞虎山遗址，出土了贵州目前唯一的一块彩陶，囿于当时的客观条件，未对遗址进行全面的发掘和研究。仅仅这一片彩陶，却大大颠覆了学术界关于彩陶文化传播范围和传播路径的既有理论，为人类沿青藏高原东麓文化传播和互动提出了新的课题。这昭示着，在中华文明形成的最初阶段，黔中地区的洞穴遗址考古学文化就已参与其中。

秦汉之际，以中原地区为中心的农耕文明集权国家建立以后，对西南地区的大规模开发逐步展开，继秦之后，汉武帝继续向贵州地区的夜郎、且兰等国开拓道路，设置郡县，汉代设立的牂牁郡就被认为设在贵州境内，汉人不仅带来了先进的生产技术，而且带来了汉文化，贵安新区分布的大量汉代墓葬，便是贵州最早开发的有力证据，根据汉代遗址墓葬的分布情况，学术界有人认为，牂牁郡郡治便位于今安顺的宁谷或今贵安新区境内的马场一带。

汉室衰微，历史进入魏晋南北朝，这个弱肉强食、朝代更迭频繁的时期，被历史学家们称为中国历史上的丛林地带。彼时，生活在黔中地区的人们，失去了中原文化的强大影响力，这一时期的各类遗存开始出现较为浓郁的地方风格，这一点在贵安新区发掘出土的魏晋墓葬中，得到充分的映证，大量珠宝和金银饰品，在同时期的汉人墓葬中极为少见，但在贵安新区境内的墓葬中却极为普遍。同时，远徙而来的汉文化顺势发展，墓葬中出土较多酒具、茶具和文房用品，显示出那个时代崇文尚玄、狂放不羁的时代风格。该批墓葬是贵州省境内少有的经过科学发掘的东晋南朝时期墓葬，为研究贵州东晋南朝时期的政治、经济、文化、社会情况，提供了重要的实物资料，具有非常重要的学术意义。这个看似混乱的年代，却是多元一体中华民族文化形成的重要时期，那时的贵安地区，即呈现出了文化的多元性和丰富性，显现出文化的多彩格局。

三、贵安考古展望

贵安考古，势头良好，发展喜人，但怎样把考古工作做得更彻底更深入？怎样让文物得到更好的保护和展示？怎样在贵安建设中更好发挥出这些成果的作用？等等问题，是摆在我们面前不容回避的。针对贵安考古资源特征和贵安建设的需要，应着重从以下方面突破和发展。

深入普查摸清家底，重点发掘揭示容颜。鉴于贵安新区行政区域性质的差异，我们的考古工作仅在核心区域做得彻底一些，而对核心区域以外的大贵安部分，做得不够彻底。下一步，要加大这部分区域工作的力度，全面摸清和掌握地下考古遗产资源的蕴藏情况。争取基本建设考古项目和贵州中西部洞穴遗址的发掘和研究五年规划在国家文物局立项，力求解决旧石器往新石器时代、狩猎往农耕文明过渡等相关学术问题；对文物分布密集的区域如马场魏晋南北朝墓地、夏云尹关墓地等，进行详细的重点钻探，确定墓葬的数量、分布范围、埋藏情况，对重点遗址区域和墓葬进行重点发掘，摸清魏晋南北朝时期该区域的文化面貌和特征，努力揭示贵安文化的历史容颜。

　　部门协调齐力并进，保护展示群芳争艳。贵安新区开发建设以来，基础设施建设速度惊人，文物部门和规划、建设部门之间要加强沟通、协调，建设项目启动之前，充分开展文物调查、勘探工作，让地下文物得到最大化的保护。广泛开展国内国际间合作，深入学术研究，多出学术成果，提升贵安品味，扩大在世界范围内的影响。公布一批区级、省级、国家级的文物保护单位，让重要文物切实纳入政府及职能部门的保护视野。辟地建设魏晋南北朝时期墓葬遗址博物馆和中国南方喀斯特洞穴遗址公园，更好地让文化遗产为文化贵安的建设服务。利用好贵州考古贵安整理基地（贵州公共考古活动中心）的职能，建成贵州最大的公共考古展示、体验和宣传基地，发挥好贵安特色考古资源的社会和经济效益。

四、结语

　　贵安考古，应该说才刚打开一扇门，而门内的长篇故事，还有待于我们考古人一锄一锄地去挖掘，贵安历史的神秘面纱，还有待于我们考古人去一层层揭开。当今的考古，已经不是象牙塔的故步自封，而在我们的学者充分建构起这一坚固的塔体后，需要向社会散发其神秘的魅力和积极的能量，除了对考古学科使命的完成，我们的研究成果，对于人类生存环境的保护、对于人类社会的可持续发展、对于文化多样性的挖掘和尊重、对于文化遗产的保护等诸多社会问题，都可以提供历史经验的借鉴和参考，让我们的贵安考古的脚步伴随贵安的发展前行。

周必素

FOREWORD

On January 6, 2014, the State Council approved to set up Guizhou Guian New District as China's eighth national district; it is endowed with three strategic positioning: the important economic growth pole in the western region, inland open economy new heights, and ecological civilization demonstration area. Guian New District includes 21 villages and towns (subdistrict offices), 312 administrative villages of Guiyang City and Anshun City, the total area is 1795 square kilometers with the population of 790000. Guian New District is located in the second step of Guizhou plateau in the middle of Guizhou hilly plain basin area, with an elevation of 1000−1500 meters. The overall regional geomorphic characteristic of this area is the wide shallow valley, the flat topography, the chain of undulating hills, and patches of intermontane basins. The most widely distributed physiognomy types in this area are the karst hills, wide karst basins, and the kegel andturm karst, etc. The climate here is a kind of subtropical wet monsoon, the annual average temperature is 18.3 °C, the average temperature in January is 6.0 °C, the average temperature of July is 23.5 °C, and the extreme minimum temperature is -7.4 °C. There are many rivers in this area, mainly including Sanchahe river, Laoyinghe river, Lepinghe river, Yangchanghe river and so on, which all belong to the Yangtze river water system. The basic morphology began to form in the period of mountain basin after the Cenozoic Himalayan orogeny. The superior natural environment gave birth to the long history and culture; it has been proven that, there was human beings lived here at least in the upper Paleolithic Age, leaving rich cultural heritage.

The Review and Main Achievements of Guian Archaeology

The archaeological work in Guian New District began in 1954, which has gone through a journey of more than 60 years.

In 1954, cultural relics of Han Dynasty were found during the process of Yangchanghe River Conservancy Project Construction, the archaeological team of the Guizhou Provincial Museum tracked the clue, and finally we found the cemetery of Han Dynasty in Guizhou for the first time, proving that the central government had begun to manage and develop here since Han Dynasty. From 1956 to 1959, we carried out large-scale archaeological arrangement for four times in the junction of Qingzhen and Pingba. The first arrangement began in the spring of 1956, 2 tombs of Han Dynasty were excavated in Jinjiadaping; the second one was in the spring of 1957, 7 tombs were excavated in Pingzhuang and Laojichang; the third one was from the middle of December, 1957 to the beginning of February, 1958, 19 tombs were excavated in Yalongba and Miaofenpo of Qingzhen; the fourth one was from December, 1958 to April, 1959, more than 140 tombs were excavated in Yinguan, Yalongba, Ludishao and Tumenzhai and so on , which are located in the junction of Qingzhen and Pingba. More than 160 tombs were excavated in these four excavations, they are of Han Dynasty to Song Dynasty, and most of them are pit tombs (3/4 or more), the rest are with stone chambers. There were a large number of pottery, porcelain, lacquer ware, bronze, gold, silver, and fabric unearthed. From 1965 to 1966, the archaeological team of Guizhou Provincial Museum excavated 34 tombs at Wanrenfen, Xiongjiapo, Dasongshan, and so on, near Machang Town of Guian New District, including 16 tombs of Eastern Jin and Southern Dynasty, and a wealth of pottery, porcelain, lacquer, copper, gold, silver and other precious relics were unearthed. In 1981, Guizhou Provincial Museum excavated Feihushan cave site at Baiyun Town, Pingba County, it was the first discovery of prehistoric cave site in Guian New District; according to the ^{14}C test, the date was about 13000 years ago, at most. A lot of stone, bone, horn, and pottery were found here, including 532 pieces of chipped stone manufacture, 21 pieces of grinding stone, 79 pieces of bone horn tools, and more than 2000 pieces of pottery.

In recent five years, with the acceleration of construction in Guian New District, in order to cooperate with the construction of Guian New District, the efforts of archaeological investigation and salvage archaeology excavations are increasing; in order to match up the infrastructure construction, field archaeological excavation and initiative archaeological work for solving the related academic problem of the prehistoric cave sites in middle and west of Guizhou advanced side by side, the archaeological work in Guian New District have developed by leaps and bounds.

In 2013, by the arrangement of Guizhou Provincial Cultural Bureau and Guizhou Provincial Administration of Cultural Heritage, Guizhou Provincial Institute of Cultural Relics and Archaeology started the census on underground cultural resources in Guian New District; on the basis of previous work, we conducted a more detailed comprehensive investigation once again. 38 cave sites of prehistoric period to Shang and Zhou Dynasties were found in Machang, Gaofeng, Huchao and Dangwu in Guian New District; besides, we also found hundreds of tombs of Western and Eastern Han Dynasties, of Wei, Jin, Southern and Northern Dynasties, of Tang, Song, Ming and Qing Dynasties. Therefore, underground cultural relics resources reserves were further found out.

In 2013, in order to cooperate with the construction of Guian New District, basic construction of archaeological work has begun on a large scale, now the work is still followed closely. According to incomplete statistics, all the construction of cultural relics survey projects we have carried out in Guian New District are about 100, including about 60 transportation construction projects, industrial parks, reservoirs, and about 40 settlements totally; we have made important gains. For example, in the construction of the road from Leizhuang to Machang, basing on the detailed investigation and exploration work in the scope of the highway construction and the surrounding areas, we found two sites of Wei, Jin, Southern and Northern Dynasties, and of Tang Dynasty in Shapo and Yangjiaqiao. It is confirmed by preliminary exploration that, there were some different periods of ancient tombs in this area. February to May, 2014, we had carried on a systematic excavation on Shapo site, and a large scale systematic exploration in Yangjiaqiao site, more than 70 ancient tombs of Wei, Jin, Southern and Northern Dynasties, and of Song and Ming Dynasties were found, 3 of them have been excavated. In 2014, to cooperate with the construction of Yingbin Avenue in Pingba, we excavated 5 tombs of Han Dynasty cemetery in Xiayun Town. There were more than 20 pieces of cultural relics unearthed, including pottery, copper, iron, silver, colored glazed, etc.

Since October 2012, Institute of Archaeology of Chinese Academy of Social Sciences, and Guizhou Provincial Institute of Cultural Relics and Archaeology carried out a five-year-lasting excavation on Niupodong site in Machang Town, the exposed area was about 90 square meters. We found 6 tombs and 6 pits here, and a large number of cultural relics with clear stratigraphic relations, including pottery, stone tools, bone artifacts and other living utensils, production tools, and stones, blocks, cores, blades, debris related to processing chipped stone tools, and also remains of water and land animals, etc. In July 2014, Guizhou Provincial Institute of Cultural Relics and Archaeology, the Archaeology Department of Sichuan University, Chengdu Municipal Institute of Cultural Relics and Archaeology carried out a small scale test excavation on Dawandong site in Machang Town. This time, most work was done outside the cave; there were 105 pieces of stoneware, and some mammal bones and a small amount of pottery unearthed. In 2016, Guizhou Provincial Institute of Cultural Relics and Archaeology, the Archaeology Department of Sichuan University, Chengdu Municipal Institute of Cultural Relics and Archaeology carried out a test excavation on Zhaoguodong site in Gaofeng Town, nearly thousands of cultural relics unearthed, including a large number of pottery, stone, bone, horn, animal bones, especially a large number of fine bone horn tools, according to the shape, they can be classified into two categories, shovel and core. Furthermore, there were a considerable number of aquatic animal bones unearthed, such as clams, snails, and fish. This site reflects that, in the upper Paleolithic Age to the early Neolithic Age, the animal resource utilization of cave dwellers in central Guizhou had reached an unprecedented breadth and depth, it also reflects the unique way of living of the low latitude plateau mountain inhabitants and their unique approach to the mountain environment; according to the profile, the accumulation of this site is very thick, so there will be a long way of research in the future.

Archaeological work was always pushed forward; meanwhile, in order to coordinate with publicity, we carried out series of public archaeology activity. In July, 2016, we organized students from Guiyang No. 1 Middle School and the archaeology club of the affiliated middle school of Guizhou Normal University to come to Zhaoguodong site in Gaofeng Town, joining in the excavation, and having experience on field excavation, making stone tools, archaeological exploration, plant flotation and so on. Affected by social popular tomb-raiding novels, students were full of curiosity for archaeological excavation work, they all considered archaeology as an exciting and mysterious business. However, via such personal feelings, they have had more practical and intuitive understanding of archaeology, and have touched more archaeological "reality"; they all recognized that, after tens of thousands of years of vicissitudes, it is very difficult to make cultural heritage remain till now; as to excavate and splice the historical debris, archaeological work is trivial, boring, even quite tough to some extent; to take the archaeological way to realize the cognition of history, we should not only show how curious we are, but also pay more hard work on it. At the same time, students felt the difference between the real experience and historical knowledge from books, felt the richness, vividness and interest of archaeology, and recognized that archaeology is a kind of knowledge to explain where humanity comes from, to help human beings finding the lost memory. This activity cultivated students' interest about archaeology—a discipline of touching the history. Taking the chance of China (Guizhou) Second International Folk Arts and Crafts Culture Products Exposition, we will hold the exhibition of archaeological results in Guian New District; it will be a good campaign for public archaeology, years of archaeological research report will be showed together, promoting the general public to get the cognition of historical culture and development of Guian New District, making archaeological achievements play better social benefit, and provide better service for Guian New District.

The Special Significance of Guian Archaeology

According to the current archaeological data which have been identified, Guian archaeology has peculiarity, uniqueness, representative and typicality in Guizhou archaeology; it does have important significance.

The low mountain hilly zone in Guian New District is the typical karst landform in south China, caves are widely distributed, thus here is the natural habitat for ancient human in Guizhou, and here is also the most concentrated distribution area of the prehistoric cave sites in Guizhou; in China and even in the world, it has the typicality and representativeness; from the point view of the density and the continuation of culture of these cave sites, here is even the most unique site. In addition, Guian New District is the only one in Guizhou with the complete sequence of archaeological remains, from the Paleolithic Age to the Ming and Qing Dynasties, here is also the only one in Guizhou which can completely write the general history by archaeology. Furthermore, the one and only piece of painted pottery of Guizhou was just found in Guian New District. It is obvious that Guian archaeology has the important significance for clearing the historical context of Guizhou and even of the southwest China.

The history of ancient human activities in Guizhou can be traced back to the middle of Pleistocene, taking Panxian Dadong site, Qianxi Guanyindong site, Tongziyan Huidong site as the representation. Guian New District is located in central Guizhou, there are many rivers distributed, so karst caves developed well, and the ecological environment is excellent; since late Pleistocene, human activities increased frequently in central Guizhou; according to the dating data of Zhaoguodong site in Gaofeng Town, 30000 − 20000 years ago, ancient human had lived in this area, they chose some caves to live, carved stones for tools, grinded bones into cones, peeled animal skins for clothes. Our ancestors sit around the fire, along with heavy knocks over and over again, at the midnight, before the dawn, they knocked on the door of the human civilization. Cave sites in Guian New District have important meaning for solving many important academic problems in the transition period between the Paleolithic Age and the Neolithic Age, such as the origin of ancient agriculture, the livestock farming, the origin of pottery; and it will play a significant role in promoting to establish the prehistoric archaeology culture sequence of Guizhou.

In 1981, the one and only piece of painted pottery of Guizhou unearthed from Feihushan site, Guian New District, constrained by the objective conditions, the site was not thoroughly explored and researched at that time. This piece of painted pottery greatly overturned the existing theory of the academia about the communication scope and propagation path of painted pottery culture, proposing the new task about people disseminate culture and interacted along the foothill of the Qinghai-Tibet plateau. This shows that the cave sites archaeological culture in central Guizhou had been involved in the initial stage of formation of Chinese civilization.

In Qin and Han Dynasties, taking the central plains area as the core, the farming civilization totalitarian state was established, after that, the large-scale development on the southwest area was gradually carried out; following Qin Dynasty, the Emperor Wu of Han Dynasty continued to break new roads, to set up prefectures and counties in Yelang, Julan, etc.; Zangke Prefecture, which was set up in Han Dynasty, was considered to be set up in Guizhou. Han nationality brought not only the advanced production technology, but also the Han culture. The large number of Han Dynasty tombs distributed in Guian New District is more evidence of the earliest development of Guizhou. According to the distribution of Han Dynasty tombs and sites, the academia argued that, the government office of Zangke Prefecture was located in Ninggu of today's Anshun, or Machang in Guian New District.

Han Dynasty was gradually decadent; the following historical period was Wei, Jin, Southern and Northern Dynasties, which was called the jungle of Chinese history due to "the law of the jungle" situation and the frequent alternation of dynasties. That time, people who lived in central Guizhou had lost the powerful influence of the central plains culture; various heritage remains began to appear strong local style in this period; this can be fully reflected by excavated tombs of Wei, Jin, Southern and Northern Dynasties in Guian New District. A large number of jewelry and gold and silver accessories are extremely common within tombs in Guian New District, but they are really rare in tombs of Han nationality at the same time. Meanwhile, the Han culture took the chance to develop, more vessels for wine, tea, and writing tools unearthed from tombs, showing the adoring literacy spirit and the wild uninhibited era style. These tombs of Wei, Jin, Southern and Northern Dynasties were excavated scientifically, it was rare in Guizhou province; and these materials provided important data for the study of political, economic, cultural, and social situation of Wei, Jin, Southern and Northern Dynasties in Guizhou; they do have very important academic significance. This seemingly chaotic period is in fact the important time of the diversity in unity of the Chinese nation's culture; at that time, Guian had presented the diversity and richness on culture, showing the colorful pattern of the culture.

The Outlook of Guian Archaeology

The momentum and development of archaeology in Guian are encouraging by now, however, how to make the archaeological work be done more thoroughly and further? How to get better protection and show of cultural relics? How to make these results play a better role in the construction of Guian? We have to face these unavoidable questions. On the characteristics of Guian archaeological resources and on the needs of Guian construction, following aspects should be focused on to get breakthrough and development.

We will take in-depth survey to clear the situation, and take key excavations to reveal the appearance. In view of the administrative regional differences of Guian New District, our archaeological work had only been carried out more in the core area, as to the rest part, it's far from enough. On the next step, we will increase the work intensity in the part outside the core area, to grasp a comprehensive understanding of the underground archaeological heritage resources reserves. We will try to get the approval by The State Administration of Cultural Heritage to set up the projects on archaeological excavation infrastructure construction, and on the five-year plan of the excavation and research on cave sites in the middle and west part of Guizhou, making efforts to solve related academic problems such as the transition from hunting civilization to farming civilization during the Paleolithic Age and the Neolithic Age. We will carry out particular exploration on areas with dense distribution of cultural relics, such as the cemetery of Wei, Jin, Southern and Northern Dynasties in Machang, and the Xiayun Yinguan cemetery, etc., making sure the number of burials, the distribution range, the burial situation; and will excavate the most important site and tombs specially to make clear appearance and features of this area in Wei, Jin, Southern and Northern Dynasties, trying to reveal the historical veil of Guian culture.

Departments will coordinate and keep pace with each other; ways of protection shows will be more various. Since Guian New District has been developed and constructed, the infrastructure construction was always at a staggering rate, therefore the cultural relics department and the department of planning and construction had better to strengthen communication and coordination, and before the construction project starting, we should fully carry out the cultural relics survey and exploration work to maximize the protection of underground cultural relics. The domestic and international cooperation should be extensively carried out, so does the in-depth academic research, thus many academic achievements will enhance the manner of Guian, and enlarge the influence worldwide. We should publish a batch of district, provincial and national cultural relics protection units, making important cultural relics be incorporated into the protect vision of the government and function departments; build the museum of burial site of Wei, Jin, Southern and Northern Dynasties and Karst Cave Site Park of south China, letting the cultural heritage offer better services for the construction of Guian; make good use of the function of Guizhou Archaeology Guian Base (Guizhou Public Archaeology Activity Center), building up the biggest base of the public archaeology for exhibition, experience and publicity in Guizhou, making archaeological resources with Guian characteristics play good social and economic benefits.

Epilogue

It should be said that, we are just opening the door of the archaeology in Guian, and a long story behind the door has yet to be told, the mystery of history has yet to be uncovered by archaeologists. Modern archaeology is not conservative in the ivory tower anymore; our scholars had fully constructed the solid tower body, basing that, we need to send out the mysterious charm and the positive energy to the society. Our research results can accomplish the archaeological mission, and also provide the historical experience and reference for the protection of human survival environment, for the sustainable development of human society, for the digging and respect on cultural diversity, for the protection of cultural heritage, and many other social problems; all above will let the archaeological steps go with the development of Guian.

ZHOU Bisu

亚洲象上臼齿

The upper molar tooth of Elephas maximus

Neolithic Age

新石器时代

2016 年马场镇牛坡洞遗址出土

单台面石核

Single platform core

Paleolithic Age

旧石器时代

长 6.75 厘米，宽 4.78 厘米，厚 4.15 厘米

2016 年马场镇扁嘴洞遗址出土

黑色，台面未加修整，保留原生石皮，剥片面残留片疤 8 个。

多台面石核
Multiple platform core
Paleolithic Age

旧石器时代
长 4.95 厘米，宽 4.71 厘米，厚 3.99 厘米
2016 年马场镇扁嘴洞遗址出土

灰褐色，台面为修整台面，共有 4 个片疤，剥片面残留片疤 13 个。

多台面石核
Multiple platform core
Paleolithic Age

旧石器时代

长 7.96 厘米，宽 7.01 厘米，厚 4.59 厘米

2016 年马场镇扁嘴洞遗址出土

黑色，台面为自然台面，保留原生石皮，剥片面残留片疤 14 个。

多台面石核
Multiple platform core
Paleolithic Age

旧石器时代

长 4.82 厘米，宽 3.74 厘米，厚 3.71 厘米

2016 年马场镇扁嘴洞遗址出土

黑色，台面共 3 个，其中修整台面 1 个，自然台面 2 个，剥片面残留片疤 11 个。

多台面石核
Multiple platform core
Paleolithic Age

旧石器时代

长 5.61 厘米，宽 3.86 厘米，厚 3.07 厘米

2016 年马场镇扁嘴洞遗址出土

黑色，台面为修整台面，共 3 个，剥片面残留片疤 7 个。

细石核
Microcore
Neolithic Age

新石器时代
长 2.11 厘米，宽 3.69 厘米，厚 1.4 厘米，重 12.7 克
2015 年马场镇牛坡洞遗址出土

黑色燧石，楔形，处于预制阶段，通体人工面，纵剖面"V"字形，基础台面为人工面，未修理，表面平整。两端皆打制修理，核体分别从台面与底缘对向打制修理；后缘与底缘均为刃状。

刮削器

Scraper

Paleolithic Age

旧石器时代
长 4.23 厘米，宽 2.77 厘米，厚 0.55 厘米
2016 年马场镇扁嘴洞遗址出土

黑色，平面形状近梯形，毛坯为石片，台面经修整，背面残留有修整痕迹，自然面比为 10%。打击泡明显，左侧可见使用形成的连续疤痕。

刮削器

Scraper
Paleolithic Age

旧石器时代
长 2.39 厘米，宽 1.37 厘米，厚 0.86 厘米
2016 年马场镇扁嘴洞遗址出土

黑色，平面形状近梯形，毛坯为石片，左右两侧均可见由腹面向背面进行的单面
加工修整痕迹，加工精致。

刮削器

Scraper

Paleolithic Age

旧石器时代

长 6.86 厘米，宽 4.25 厘米，厚 2.67 厘米

2016 年马场镇扁嘴洞遗址出土

黑色，平面形状呈扇形，毛坯为石片，背面残留部分石皮，台面未加修整，打击
点清晰，远端经双面加工修整成为刃缘，刃缘呈锯齿状。

刮削器

Scraper

Paleolithic Age

旧石器时代

长 4.15 厘米，宽 2.8 厘米，厚 1.8 厘米

2016 年马场镇扁嘴洞遗址出土

黑色，平面形状近梯形，毛坯为石片，背面残留部分石皮，台面未加修整，远端和右侧均可见由腹面向背面进行的单面加工修整痕迹。

刮削器

Scraper

Paleolithic Age

旧石器时代

长 4.98 厘米，宽 3.72 厘米，厚 2.07 厘米

2016 年马场镇扁嘴洞遗址出土

黑色，平面形状近椭圆形，毛坯为石片，背面残留部分石皮，腹面经后期打制修整，原打击痕迹已不可见，左右两侧均可见加工修整痕迹，均为双面加工，加工精致。

刮削器

Scraper

Paleolithic Age

旧石器时代

长 8.66 厘米，宽 6.05 厘米，厚 2.15 厘米

2016 年马场镇扁嘴洞遗址出土

黑色，平面形状呈不规则形，毛坯为石片，石料节理发达，可见两处加工修整痕迹，其中下端可见由腹面向背面进行的单面加工痕迹，右侧为双面加工，加工较粗糙。

刮削器

Scraper

Neolithic Age

新石器时代

长 4.69 厘米，宽 2.54 厘米，厚 1.44 厘米

2016 年高峰镇招果洞遗址出土

灰白色，平面形状呈梯形，毛坯为石片，修理痕迹清晰，除近端外其余三侧均经后期加工修整形成刃缘，加工方向以腹面向背面为主，右侧可见零星的双面加工痕迹，左侧经仔细修整呈锯齿状，加工精致。

刮削器

Scraper

Neolithic Age

新石器时代

长 4.48 厘米，宽 2.76 厘米，厚 1.58 厘米

2016 年高峰镇招果洞遗址出土

黑色，毛坯为石片，自然台面，远端可见双面修整痕迹，形成刃缘，刃缘呈锯齿状，加工精致。

刮削器

Scraper

Neolithic Age

新石器时代
长 2.96 厘米，宽 2.47 厘米，厚 0.96 厘米
2016 年高峰镇招果洞遗址出土

黑色，平面呈不规则形，毛坯为石片，台面为修整台面，右侧可见双面加工修整痕迹，形成刃缘，左侧可见从腹面向背面进行的单面加工修整痕迹。

刮削器

Scraper

Neolithic Age

新石器时代

长 3.04 厘米，宽 3 厘米，厚 0.67 厘米

2016 年高峰镇招果洞遗址出土

黑色，平面形状近梯形，毛坯为石片，对腹面进行减薄加工，在此基础上修整背面台面，对背面进行减薄处理，左侧可见从腹面向背面进行的单面加工修整痕迹，形成刃缘。

刮削器
Scraper
Neolithic Age

新石器时代

长 4 厘米，宽 2.57 厘米，厚 1.08 厘米

2016 年高峰镇招果洞遗址出土

黑色，平面形状近梯形，毛坯为石片，背面残留部分石皮，台面经后期修整，打击点已不可见，右侧可见由腹面向背面进行的单面加工修整痕迹，形成刃缘。

刮削器

Scraper

Neolithic Age

新石器时代

长 2.85 厘米，宽 2.49 厘米，厚 0.81 厘米

2016 年高峰镇招果洞遗址出土

灰色，平面形状近梯形，毛坯为石片，左右两侧可见由背面向腹面进行的单面加工痕迹，加工较精致。

刮削器

Scraper

Neolithic Age

新石器时代

长 3.07 厘米，宽 2.44 厘米，厚 1.05 厘米

2016 年高峰镇招果洞遗址出土

黑色，平面形状近梯形，毛坯为石片，台面经过修整，打击点不可见，远端可见单面加工修整痕迹，形成较为明显的刃缘，刃缘呈锯齿状。

砍砸器

Chopper

Neolithic Age

新石器时代
长 8.61 厘米，宽 9.37 厘米，厚 3.57 厘米，重 340.32 克
2013 年马场镇牛坡洞遗址出土

灰白色灰岩，平面形状近长方形，利用砾石制成，器表残留大面积自然石皮，一端单向打击出尖锐的刃缘，有使用痕迹，另一端亦经过打击，较钝。

砍砸器

Chopper

Neolithic Age

新石器时代
长 6.68 厘米，宽 4.79 厘米，厚 3.54 厘米，重 116.54 克
2013 年马场镇牛坡洞遗址出土

黑色燧石，以砾石为毛坯，单向修整，修疤连续叠压分布，刃缘不规则。

砍砸器

Chopper
Neolithic Age

新石器时代

长 7.56 厘米，宽 7.13 厘米，厚 3.4 厘米，重 303.24 克

2013 年马场镇牛坡洞遗址出土

灰色粉砂岩，平面形状近长方形，利用砾石制成，在两个平面的中部各有一个对称的近圆形浅凹窝，四周有明显砸击形成的坑疤，其中一端非常明显。

石锤

Hammerstone
Neolithic Age

新石器时代

长 7 厘米，宽 3.7 厘米，厚 2.2 厘米，重 578.2 克

1981 年平坝县飞虎山遗址出土

椭圆形，毛坯为扁圆形砾石，两面扁平，扁平面两侧中心加工呈凹坑，两侧凹坑对称，略呈圆形，直径为 2.5 厘米，上大下小，凹坑底部有打击痕迹。

细石叶
Microblade
Neolithic Age

新石器时代
长 2.32 厘米，宽 0.77 厘米，厚 0.31 厘米，重 0.5 克
2014 年马场镇牛坡洞遗址出土

黑色燧石，平面呈长方形，点状台面，打击点清晰，可见波纹，背面有两个同向片疤，一条纵脊，两侧边平行，侧缘薄锐，截面呈三角形，远端薄锐。

细石叶
Microblade
Neolithic Age

新石器时代
长 2.73 厘米，宽 0.93 厘米，厚 0.52 厘米，重 0.74 克
2014 年马场镇牛坡洞遗址出土

黑色燧石，平面呈倒三角形，不规则素台面，可见唇，其余人工特征不明显，背面有两个同向片疤和一条纵脊，两侧边平行，侧缘薄锐，截面呈三角形，远端尖灭。

磨石

Abrader

Neolithic Age

新石器时代

长 6.05 厘米，宽 4.11 厘米，厚 1.41 厘米

2016 年高峰镇招果洞遗址出土

黄褐色，磨制痕迹明显，中间薄，四周较厚，呈凹透镜形状。

磨制石器

Ground stone

Neolithic Age

新石器时代

长 4.33 厘米，宽 4.31 厘米，厚 1.07 厘米

2016 年高峰镇招果洞遗址出土

青灰色，破损严重，磨制精致，可能为石斧或石锛近刃部残片。

磨制石器

Ground stone

Neolithic Age

新石器时代

长 7.3 厘米，宽 4.27 厘米，厚 3.25 厘米，重 190.5 克

2013 年马场镇牛坡洞遗址出土

以花岗岩砾石为毛坯，一端残断，另一端疑似有砸击形成的崩疤，其余面均经过打磨。

磨制石器

Ground stone

Neolithic Age

新石器时代

长 8.31 厘米，宽 8.81 厘米，厚 2.95 厘米，重 400.86 克

2013 年马场镇牛坡洞遗址出土

灰色粉砂岩，横截面呈椭圆形，两端残断，其余面打磨精致。

磨制石器
Ground stone
Neolithic Age

新石器时代
长 9.84 厘米，宽 7.19 厘米，厚 3.46 厘米，重 430.65 克
2013 年马场镇牛坡洞遗址出土

灰绿色粉砂岩，器身长方形，通体磨制精细，顶端可见少量修疤，两侧磨制圆钝，器形规整。刃部两面不对称，一面略陡，一面略缓。刃缘可见少量使用崩疤。

磨制石器
Ground stone
Neolithic Age

新石器时代
长 5.34 厘米，宽 5.51 厘米，厚 2.29 厘米，重 107.62 克
2013 年马场镇牛坡洞遗址出土

灰色石英岩，通体磨制精细，残余刃端，两侧磨制圆钝，器形规整，刃部磨制精细。刃部两面对称，正锋。

石锛
Stone Adze
Neolithic Age

新石器时代

长 6.5 厘米，刃宽 4.9 厘米，厚 1.4 厘米，重 97.9 克

1981 年平坝县飞虎山遗址出土

米乳色，石质颇细，长方形，下宽上窄，一面开刃。

石锛
Stone Adze
Neolithic Age

新石器时代

长 5 厘米，刃宽 4.9 厘米，厚 1.4 厘米，重 432.5 克

1981 年平坝县飞虎山遗址出土

灰岩，长方形，下宽上窄，一面开刃。

石斧

Stone Axe

Neolithic Age

新石器时代
长 9 厘米，刃宽 6.3 厘米，厚 1.5 厘米，重 330.1 克
1981 年平坝县飞虎山遗址出土

长方形，上窄下宽，两面圆弧，刃宽，石质细，表面多斑点。

石矛
Stone Spear
Neolithic Age

新石器时代
长 9 厘米，宽 3.2 厘米，重 26.7 克
1981 年平坝县飞虎山遗址出土

柳叶形等腰三角状，体扁薄，两面中间均有宽凹槽以便于固定，锋部有缺口。

石镞
Stone Arrow
Neolithic Age

新石器时代
长 5 厘米，宽 1.7 厘米，重 5.9 克
1981 年平坝县飞虎山遗址出土

暗红色，长方上尖形，上尖底平，中厚边薄，下部长方形，上端双收成尖。

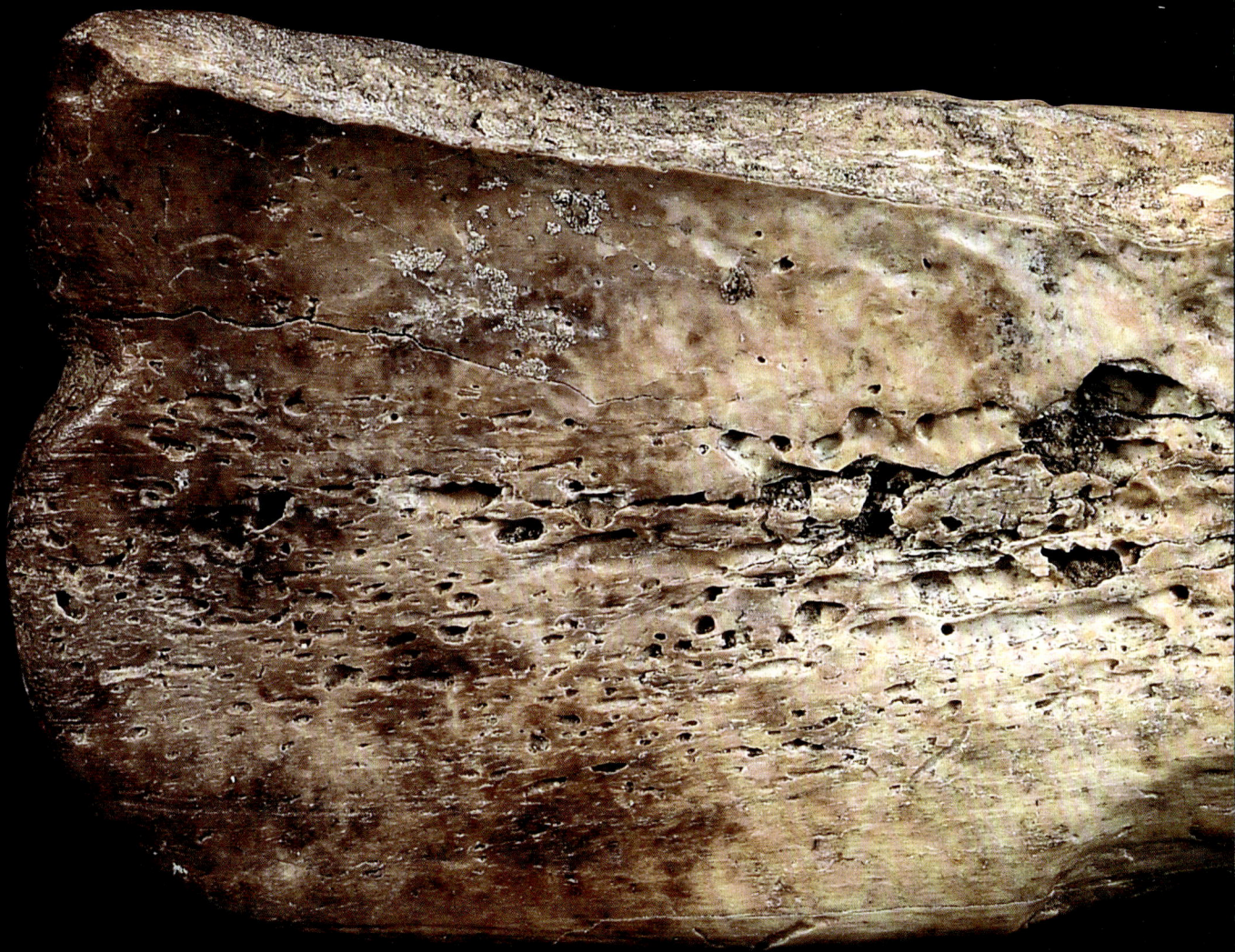

骨铲
Bone Shovel
Neolithic Age

新石器时代

长 12.7 厘米，宽 3.5 厘米，厚 1.2 厘米

2016 年高峰镇招果洞遗址出土

以骨片制成，一端经单面磨制形成圆刃，一端经双面加工形成偏刃，刃部可见使用过程中产生的崩疤。

骨铲

Bone Shovel

Neolithic Age

新石器时代

长 12.9 厘米，宽 2.9 厘米，厚 0.7 厘米

2016 年高峰镇招果洞遗址出土

以骨片制成，一端经单面磨制形成偏刃，另一端残损严重，仅可见一侧刃角，中部胶结有鱼刺。

骨铲
Bone Shovel
Neolithic Age

新石器时代
长 11.7 厘米，宽 4.1 厘米，厚 1.1 厘米
2016 年高峰镇招果洞遗址出土

以骨片制成，两端经仔细磨制形成刃部，一侧为圆刃，一侧为偏刃，刃部可见磨制产生的密集擦痕。

骨铲

Bone Shovel

Neolithic Age

新石器时代

长 12.9 厘米，宽 3.7 厘米，厚 1.1 厘米

2016 年高峰镇招果洞遗址出土

以骨片制成，单面磨制形成刃部，刃部残损严重，磨制极精致，通体可见磨制产生的擦痕，骨铲残留有烧制痕迹。

骨铲
Bone Shovel

Neolithic Age

新石器时代

长 7.9 厘米，宽 2.9 厘米，厚 0.7 厘米

2016 年高峰镇招果洞遗址出土

以骨片制成，中部折断，圆刃，磨制极其精致，刃部可见使用过程中产生的崩疤，崩疤被其后的磨制痕迹覆盖，为多次使用的骨铲。

骨铲
Bone Shovel
Neolithic Age

新石器时代
长 7.1 厘米，宽 2.9 厘米，厚 0.6 厘米
2016 年高峰镇招果洞遗址出土

以骨片制成，中部折断，经双面磨制呈平直刃，刃部可见使用过程中产生的崩疤，骨铲残留有烧制痕迹。

骨铲

Bone Shovel

Neolithic Age

新石器时代

长 7 厘米，宽 2.7 厘米，厚 0.9 厘米

2016 年高峰镇招果洞遗址出土

以骨片制成，刃部经两面磨制呈直刃，刃部可见使用过程中产生的崩疤，骨铲破损严重，中部折断，并沿长轴折断。

骨铲
Bone Shovel
Neolithic Age

新石器时代
长 8.7 厘米，宽 3.9 厘米，厚 1.2 厘米
2016 年高峰镇招果洞遗址出土

以骨片制成，风化严重，经单侧磨制形成平直刃。

骨锥

Bone Awl
Neolithic Age

新石器时代

长 10.7 厘米，宽 2.2 厘米，厚 0.5 厘米

2016 年高峰镇招果洞遗址出土

以骨片制成，破损严重，沿长轴折断，刃部仅余一侧刃角、磨制极精致。

长 12.8 厘米，宽 1.7 厘米，厚 0.6 厘米
2016 年高峰镇招果洞遗址出土

以骨片制成，尖头部呈锐角三角形体，夹角较小，尖头部分经仔细磨制，尖端较圆滑。

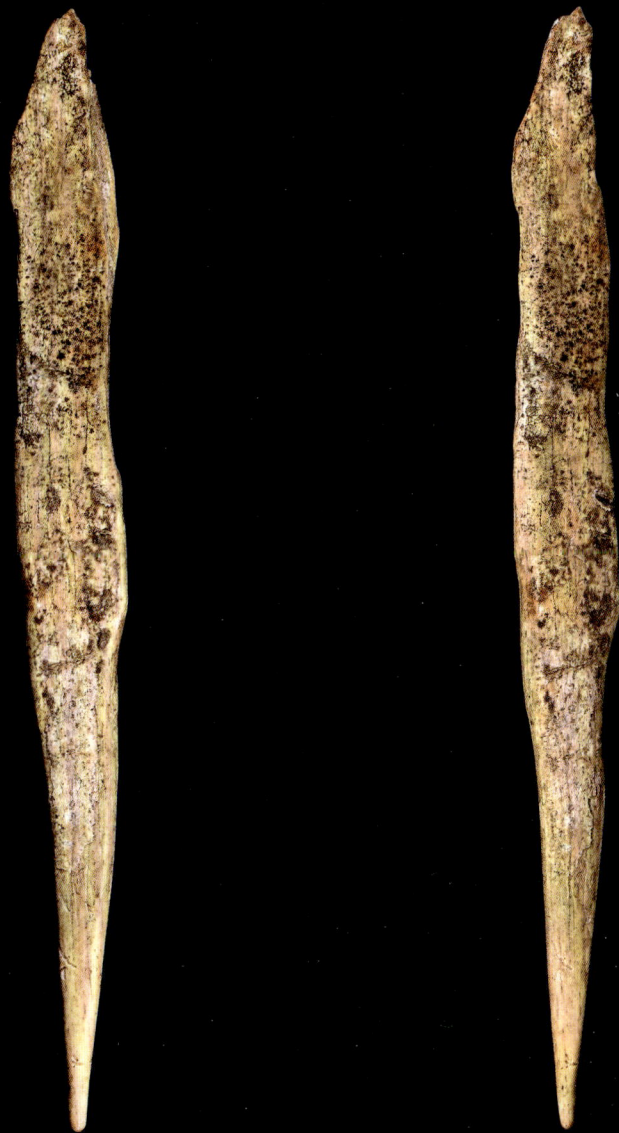

角铲

Horn Shovel

Neolithic Age

新石器时代

长 12.3 厘米，宽 3.3 厘米，厚 1.7 厘米

2016 年高峰镇招果洞遗址出土

以鹿角制成，一端经双面磨制形成偏刃，柄部未见加工痕迹。

角铲

Horn Shovel

Neolithic Age

新石器时代

长 12.2 厘米，宽 2.4 厘米，厚 1 厘米

2016 年高峰镇招果洞遗址出土

以鹿角制成，一端经双面磨制形成偏刃，一端经单面磨制形成圆刃。

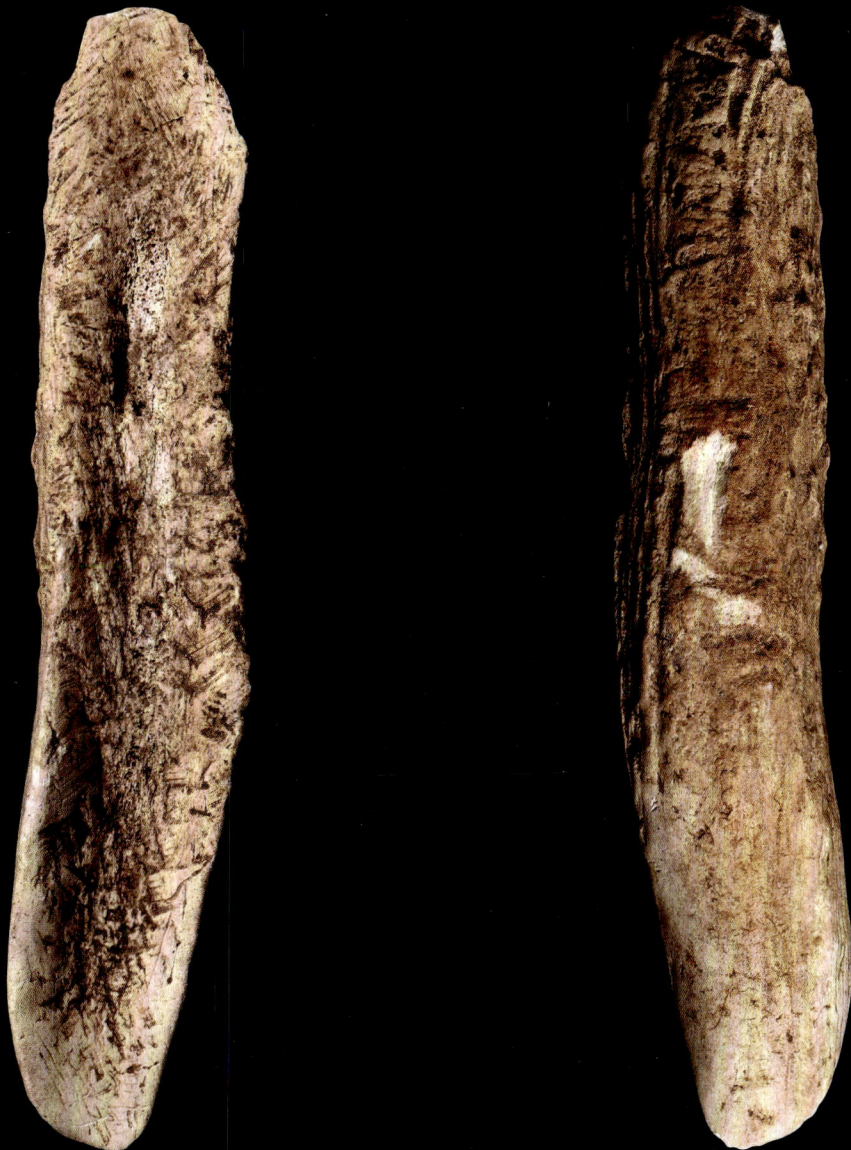

角铲

Horn Shovel

Neolithic Age

新石器时代

长 10.6 厘米，宽 3.2 厘米，厚 0.6 厘米

2016 年高峰镇招果洞遗址出土

以鹿角制成（种属未鉴定），一端经双面磨制形成偏刃，中部破损严重，刃部可见使用过程中产生的崩疤。

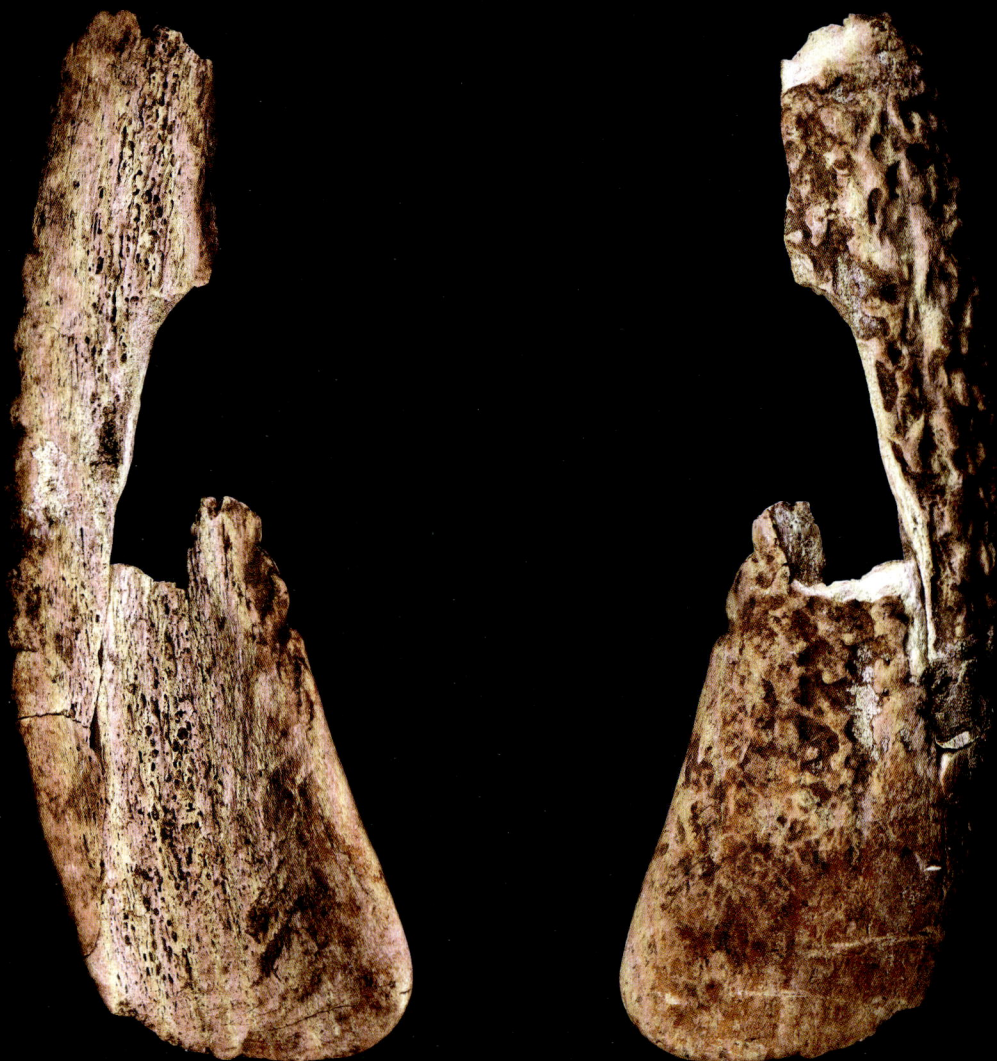

角铲

Horn Shovel

Neolithic Age

新石器时代
长 13.2 厘米，宽 2.4 厘米，厚 0.6 厘米
2016 年高峰镇招果洞遗址出土

以鹿角制成，一端经双面磨制形成圆刃，中部折断，刃部可见使用过程中产生的崩疤。

角锥

Horn Awl

Neolithic Age

新石器时代

长 14.5 厘米，最大径 2.9 厘米

2016 年高峰镇招果洞遗址出土

由鹿角制成，呈半圆锥体，通体均经过仔细磨制，顶部可见折断痕迹，底端可见加工砍砸痕迹。

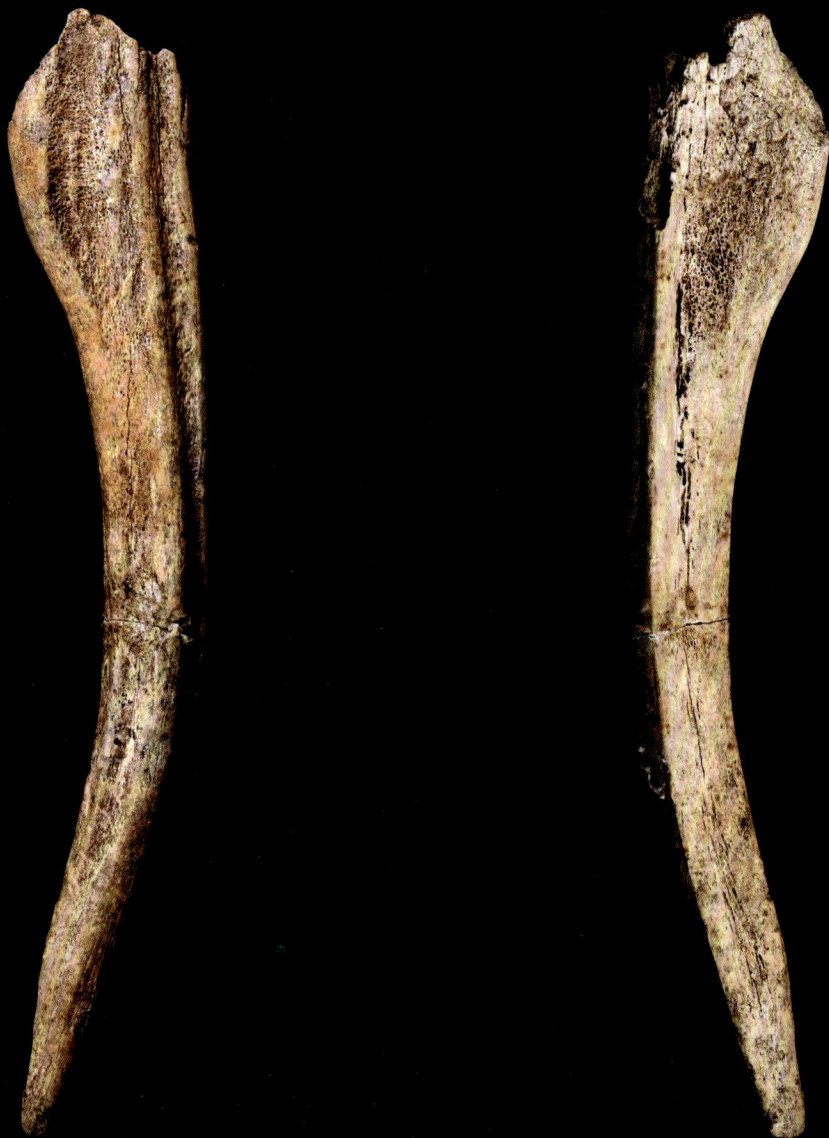

角锥

Horn Awl

Neolithic Age

新石器时代
长 31.6 厘米，最大径 4.1 厘米
2016 年高峰镇招果洞遗址出土

由鹿角制成，呈圆锥体，鹿角上部经仔细磨制，顶部完好，未见使用痕迹，下端
残损严重。

角锥

Horn Awl

Neolithic Age

新石器时代
长 28.5 厘米，最大径 3.7 厘米
2016 年高峰镇招果洞遗址出土

由鹿角制成，呈圆锥体，仅近顶部经仔细磨制，顶部可见使用过程中产生的崩疤。

彩陶陶片

Painted pottery shard

Neolithic Age

新石器时代

残长 4 厘米，宽 3.5 厘米

1981 年平坝县飞虎山遗址出土

上面绘有彩色纹饰，另有米点纹刻划符号。

陶罐

Pottery *guan* jar

Neolithic Age

新石器时代
2014 年马场镇牛坡洞遗址出土
高 24.9 厘米，口径 15.6 厘米，底径 10.4 厘米

夹砂灰陶，内壁黑色。圆唇，深腹，平底，近唇部饰竖向
绳纹，肩部绳纹呈横向，肩部以下饰交错绳纹。

陶罐

Pottery guan jar

Han Dynasty

汉

高 26.1 厘米，口径 14.4 厘米，底径 17 厘米

1954 年平坝县金银金家大坪平 M2 出土

泥质细，表面带白黄色。直口，口外有一棱，圆鼓腹，平底，
肩上饰一周锯齿纹。

陶罐

Pottery *guan* jar

Han Dynasty

汉

高 25.4 厘米，口径 11.9 厘米，底径 17.2 厘米

1956 年平坝县马场汉墓出土

泥质灰陶。直口，尖唇，束颈，腹部略鼓，平底。下腹部刻有隶书铭文 33 字，为"永元十六年正月廿五日为古沉，四耳包面，小口，中可都酒，行贺吉祠。古沉直金廿五。"

陶罐

Pottery *guan* jar

Han Dynasty

汉

高 21.7 厘米，口径 17.5 厘米，底径 20.1 厘米

1966 年平坝县天龙大小山 M70 出土

泥质红陶。口微向外侈，尖唇，唇斜外折，椭圆腹，平底，最大腹上印有小方格纹间以方形几何纹。

陶罐

Pottery *guan* jar

Han Dynasty

汉

高 22.1 厘米，口径 16.2 厘米，腹径 21.2 厘米，底径
18.1 厘米

2014 年平坝县夏云尹关、母猪龙潭汉墓群 M79 出土

泥质红陶。侈口，尖唇，短颈，腹略鼓，平底，肩腹饰方格纹。

陶罐

Pottery *guan* jar

Han Dynasty

汉

高 10 厘米，口径 12.5 厘米，最大腹径 14.8 厘米，底径 9.7 厘米

2014 年平坝县夏云尹关、母猪龙潭汉墓群 M78 出土

泥质白陶，陶质坚硬。侈口，圆唇，高领，短颈，折腹，最大腹径位于腹部转折处，上腹微鼓，下腹斜收，平底，上腹部饰两周凹弦纹。

陶罐

Pottery *guan* jar

Han Dynasty

汉

高 21.4 厘米，口径 15.5 厘米，最大腹径 22.3 厘米，底径
17.2 厘米

2014 年平坝县夏云尹关、母猪龙潭汉墓群 M78 出土

泥质红陶，局部灰色。大口，直沿，圆唇，短颈，溜肩，直腹，
大平底，四耳，肩腹部饰方格纹和凹弦纹。

陶罐

Pottery *guan* jar

Han Dynasty

汉

高 25.5 厘米，口径 13.5 厘米，最大腹径 28.8 厘米，底径 18 厘米

2014 年平坝县夏云尹关、母猪龙潭汉墓群 M79 出土

泥质灰陶，质地松软。口微侈，唇下内收形成窄沿，尖唇，短颈，平肩，鼓腹，最大腹径位于上腹部，平底，肩部饰两周压印纹。

陶罐

Pottery *guan* jar

Han Dynasty

汉
高 10.8 厘米，口径 7.9 厘米，最大腹径 11.7 厘米
2014 年平坝县夏云尹关、母猪龙潭汉墓群 M79 出土

夹粗砂灰褐陶，陶质较差，火候较低。侈口，圆唇，短颈略收，鼓腹，圜底，有单耳，耳扁平，耳上部接于颈部，下部接于腹部，上部略窄，向下逐渐变宽，局部饰粗绳纹。

陶罐

Pottery *guan* jar
Han Dynasty

汉

高 21.7 厘米，口径 15.7 厘米，最大腹径 20.8 厘米，底径 17.8 厘米

2014 年平坝县夏云尹关、母猪龙潭汉墓群 M80 出土

泥质红陶。侈口，尖唇，短颈，腹略鼓，平底，肩腹部饰方格纹。

陶罐

Pottery *guan* jar

Han Dynasty

汉

高 20.4 厘米，口径 13.6 厘米，最大腹径 23.1 厘米，底径 14.5 厘米

2014 年平坝县夏云尹关、母猪龙潭汉墓群 M80 出土

泥质灰陶，陶质松软。侈口，方唇，短颈，鼓腹，最大腹径位于上腹部，平底，上腹部有两道凸起。

陶罐

Pottery *guan* jar

Han Dynasty

汉

高 9.6 厘米，口径 9.1 厘米，最大腹径 12.7 厘米，底径 8.4
厘米

2014 年平坝县夏云尹关、母猪龙潭汉墓群 M80 出土

泥质灰陶，陶质坚硬。侈口，尖唇，短颈，鼓腹，平底，
上腹部饰两周凹弦纹。

陶罐

Pottery *guan* jar

Han Dynasty

汉

高 26.4 厘米，口径 9.4 厘米，最大腹径 24.3 厘米，底径 13.5 厘米

2014 年平坝县夏云尹关、母猪龙潭汉墓群 M80 出土

泥质灰陶，陶质松软。口微侈，唇下内收形成窄沿，圆唇，短颈，鼓腹，最大腹径位于上腹部，平底。

陶罐

Pottery *guan* jar

Han Dynasty

汉

高 8.5 厘米，口径 6.8 厘米，最大腹径 11.7 厘米

2014 年平坝县夏云尹关、母猪龙潭汉墓群 M81 出土

夹粗砂黄褐陶，陶质较差，火候较低，肩部有明显的拼接痕迹。侈口，圆唇，短颈略收，鼓腹，圜底，有单耳，耳扁平，耳上部接于颈部，下部接于腹部，宽 2.4 厘米。

釉陶罐

Glazed pottery *guan* jar

Han Dynasty

汉

高 10.8 厘米，口径 9.1 厘米，最大腹径 13.8 厘米，底径 8.3 厘米

2014 年平坝县夏云尹关、母猪龙潭汉墓群 M78 出土

胎白色，陶质坚硬，表面施酱色釉，局部脱落。口微侈，唇下内收形成窄沿，尖唇，折腹，上腹微鼓，下腹斜收，平底略内凹，上腹部饰两周凹弦纹。

釉陶罐

Glazed pottery *guan* jar

Han Dynasty

汉

高 11.6 厘米，口径 8.5 厘米，最大腹径 15.7 厘米，底径 11.2 厘米

2014 年平坝县夏云尹关、母猪龙潭汉墓群 M78 出土

泥质红陶，局部灰色，通体施青釉，釉层较薄，局部脱落。直口，圆唇，短颈，鼓肩，腹微鼓，平底略内凹，唇下有一周凸起的棱，肩部有两个对称的系，并有一周凹弦纹。

釉陶罐

Glazed pottery *guan* jar

Han Dynasty

汉

高 20 厘米，口径 15 厘米，最大腹径 20.8 厘米，底径
16.3 厘米

2014 年平坝县夏云尹关、母猪龙潭汉墓群 M80 出土

泥质红陶，通体施酱釉。直口，圆唇，短颈，腹微鼓，平底，
肩腹部饰拍印方格纹，下腹部素面。

釉陶罐

Glazed pottery *guan* jar

Han Dynasty

汉

高 21.7 厘米，口径 14.6 厘米，最大腹径 21.3 厘米，底径 17.2 厘米

2014 年平坝县夏云尹关、母猪龙潭汉墓群 M80 出土

泥质灰褐陶，上腹部施黄褐色釉。口微侈，圆唇，短颈略收，肩部平均对称分布四系，腹微鼓，最大腹径位于上腹部，平底略内凹，肩部和腹部各饰一周凹弦纹。

釉陶罐

Glazed pottery *guan* jar

Han Dynasty

汉

高 20 厘米，口径 15 厘米，最大腹径 20.8 厘米，底径
16.3 厘米

2014 年平坝县夏云尹关、母猪龙潭汉墓群 M80 出土

泥质灰陶，通体施青釉，釉层较薄，局部脱落。直口，圆唇，
短颈，鼓肩，腹微鼓，平底略内凹，唇下有一周凸起的棱，
肩部两个对称桥形系，过耳饰一周凹弦纹。

釉陶壶

Glazed pottery *hu* pot

Han Dynasty

汉

高 29 厘米，口径 11.9 厘米，最大腹径 21.5 厘米，足径 12.3 厘米

2014 年平坝县夏云尹关、母猪龙潭汉墓群 M78 出土

泥质黄褐陶，圈足以上器身表面施酱釉，局部脱落，器身有明显的轮制痕迹。直口，方唇，长颈，鼓腹，高圈足，颈肩部有对称铺首衔环耳。

釉陶豆

Glazed pottery *dou* food container

Han Dynasty

汉

高 7.1 厘米，口径 9.1 厘米，足径 5.4 厘米

2014 年平坝县夏云尹关、母猪龙潭汉墓群 M78 出土

泥质黄褐陶，圈足以上器身施酱釉，釉层不均匀，局部脱落。整体较矮胖，直口，圆唇，唇下有一周凸起的棱，豆盘较深，略鼓，短柄，圈足。

釉陶量

Glazed pottery *liang* measure

Han Dynasty

汉

高 5.3 厘米，口径 7 厘米，底径 4.3 厘米

1959 年清镇县芦狄新新桥清 M57 出土

泥质灰陶，青釉，局部脱落。敛口，口沿外侈，高领，圆腹，平底，腹上有弦纹。

陶罐

Pottery *guan* jar

Wei, Jin, Northern and Southern Dynasties

魏晋南北朝

高 14.2 厘米，口径 9.8 厘米，最大腹径
14.6 厘米，底径 11.3 厘米

2014 年马场镇杨家桥遗址 M1 出土

泥质灰陶。口微外敞，尖唇，肩上四桥形系，
下腹内收，大平底，肩腹部饰弦纹。出土时，
上盖石块。

陶罐

Pottery *guan* jar

Wei, Jin, Northern and Southern Dynasties

魏晋南北朝

高 15.9 厘米，口径 10.1 厘米，最大腹径 15.6 厘米，底
径 11.9 厘米

2014 年马场镇杨家桥遗址 M1 出土

泥质灰陶。口微敞，尖唇，肩上四桥形系，下腹内收，大平底，
肩腹部饰凹弦纹。

陶罐

Pottery *guan* jar

Wei, Jin, Northern and Southern Dynasties

魏晋南北朝

高 24.5 厘米，口径 16.5 厘米，底径 19 厘米，重 3.78
千克

1965 年平坝县马场万人坟平 M34 出土

泥质黄陶，表面涂黑色。口唇直，口下有四个对称四桥系，
平底。

釉陶罐

Glazed pottery *guan* jar
Wei, Jin, Northern and Southern Dynasties

魏晋南北朝

高 28 厘米，口径 19.3 厘米，底径 23.5 厘米，重 7.12 千克
1954 年平坝县夏云尹关平 M9 出土

泥质灰陶，器内外施青釉，开鱼片纹，过耳有隐弦纹二周。基本完整，口部缺损修复。直口，口起一沿，无颈，腹上耸，圆鼓腹，腹下至底敛，平底，腹上有桥形六系，两只竖置，四只横置。

釉陶罐

Glazed pottery *guan* jar

Wei, Jin, Northern and Southern Dynasties

魏晋南北朝

高 12.3 厘米，口径 9.8 厘米，底径 12 厘米，重 987.5 克

1954 年平坝县夏云尹关平 M9 出土

泥质灰陶，口、肩及上腹部施酱釉。微残，三耳残，两耳修补，口修补。直口，圆鼓腹，平底，底心微上凸，四泥条耳置腹上。过耳有两周隐弦纹，耳上即胸有一道凸棱纹，口沿亦饰有弦纹。

釉陶兽水盂
Monster-shaped glazed pottery *shuiyu* water pot
Wei, Jin, Northern and Southern Dynasties

魏晋南北朝
高 8.6 厘米，口径 2.6 厘米，通长 11.8 厘米，重 124.6 克
1957 年平坝县夏云尹关 M9 出土

泥质灰陶，青釉，开鱼片纹，釉剥蚀已剩无几。兽作狮形，
昂首站立，全身毛发卷曲，形态生动雄浑，狮背一长颈口。

瓷罐

Porcelain *guan* jar
Wei, Jin, Northern and Southern Dynasties

魏晋南北朝

罐高 15 厘米，口径 6.7 厘米，底径 9.1 厘米，重 884.2 克；
盘高 2.9 厘米，口径 13 厘米

1965 年平坝县马场万人坟平 M34 出土

青釉从口下直至底上，有明显釉淌横。罐身略有损纹，盘
口稍缺损。罐，口唇直，桥形六系，腹下敛，底平。盘，
敞口，圜底。出土时盘反扣在罐口上，作为罐盖，盘也可
单独使用。

瓷罐

Porcelain *guan* jar

Wei, Jin, Northern and Southern Dynasties

魏晋南北朝

高 20.5 厘米，口径 14 厘米，最大腹径 22.2 厘米，底径 15 厘米，重 3100.7 克

1965 年平坝县马场万人坟平 M34 出土

釉施至腹下部，青黄色开片，釉色莹润。直口，无颈，圆鼓腹，平底，肩上置六个桥形系，已残，肩部饰两周凸弦纹，弦纹下堆塑双层倒垂莲花瓣，每层十一瓣，花瓣直垂腹下，瓣尖略微上卷。此器造型优美，塑工精湛生动。

瓷罐

Porcelain *guan* jar

Wei, Jin, Northern and Southern Dynasties

魏晋南北朝

高 23.5 厘米，口径 12.2 厘米，底径 6 厘米，重 2956.7 克

1965 年平坝县马场万人坟平 M34 出土

青釉。口唇直，口下桥形六系，四系横置，二系竖置，椭圆腹上鼓下收，平底。

瓷罐

Porcelain *guan* jar

Wei, Jin, Northern and Southern Dynasties

魏晋南北朝

高 8.6 厘米，口径 7.7 厘米，底径 7.5 厘米，重 345.7 克

1965 年平坝县马场万人坟平 M34 出土

胎白色，上有青黄釉至腹下部，釉已大部分剥落，腹以上仍显褐色釉圆点饰，过耳釉下有一周凹弦纹。器形矮小，腹上部有桥形四系。

瓷罐

Porcelain *guan* jar

Wei, Jin, Northern and Southern Dynasties

魏晋南北朝

高 22 厘米，口径 10.8 厘米，底径 18.7 厘米，重 3.22
千克

1965 年平坝县马场万人坟平 M38 出土

全身内外壁均呈黄绿色开片釉，釉已部分脱落，过耳釉下
有一周凹弦纹。直口，圆唇，肩上有四桥形系，椭圆腹，
平底。

瓷罐

Porcelain *guan* jar

Wei, Jin, Northern and Southern Dynasties

魏晋南北朝

高 26 厘米，口径 12 厘米，底径 17 厘米，重 3.7 千克

1965 年平坝县马场熊家坡平 M48 出土

内外均施黄绿釉，腹下釉痕成行，釉下一周划花双层莲花瓣绕腹上，过耳釉下有两周凹弦纹。直口，折肩，肩上置桥形六系，四横两竖，圆鼓腹，下腹敛，平底。

瓷带盖罐

Porcelain *guan* jar with cover

Wei, Jin, Northern and Southern Dynasties

魏晋南北朝

通高 8.4 厘米，口径 10 厘米，最大腹径 12.8 厘米，底
径 7 厘米，重 452.4 克

1965 年平坝县马场熊家坡平 M50 出土

盖外与罐内外均施淡绿色釉，盖外表有褐色斑点。微残，
盖纽残缺，盖耳残。罐，短直口，桥形四系，圆扁腹，底
作实圈足，过耳釉下有一周凹弦纹。盖，圆凸顶，桥形系，
凸起外有十四条齿纹，沿饰三周凹弦纹，内沿有一周凸起
子母口沿。

瓷盘口壶

Porcelain *hu* pot with disc-shaped mouth
Wei, Jin, Northern and Southern Dynasties

魏晋南北朝
高 36 厘米，口径 9.2 厘米，底径 17.6 厘米，重 6.72 千克
1965 年平坝县马场万人坟平 M38 出土

全身呈深褐色开片釉，现已大部分脱落，过耳釉下有两周凹弦纹。直口，肩上六系耳（两耳残），圆鼓腹很大，平底。

瓷鸡首壶

Porcelain *hu* pot with cock-shaped spout
Wei, Jin, Northern and Southern Dynasties

魏晋南北朝

高 44.8 厘米，口径 12.5 厘米，底径 19.3 厘米，重 10.5 千克

1965 年平坝县马场万人坟平 M48 出土

青釉。微残，盘口残缺，鸡冠缺损。盘口，细颈，肩上置桥形系，椭圆腹，平底，流作鸡首形，过耳隐两周凹弦纹。

瓷碗

Porcelain *wan* bowl

Wei, Jin, Northern and Southern Dynasties

魏晋南北朝
高 4.5 厘米，口径 8.3 厘米，足径 5.2 厘米，重 141.8 克
1965 年平坝县马场万人坟平 M38 出土

全身呈黄绿色开片釉。略敛口，尖唇，圈足。

瓷碗

Porcelain *wan* bowl

Wei, Jin, Northern and Southern Dynasties

魏晋南北朝
高 7.6 厘米，口径 13.2 厘米，足径 4.6 厘米，重 372.2 克
1965 年平坝县马场大松山平 M55 出土

内外施黄绿釉，显龟裂纹，碗底粘少量漆皮。直口，圈足，
口沿釉下隐两周凹弦纹。

陶罐

Pottery *guan* jar
Tang Dynasty

唐

高 32.4 厘米，口径 19.6 厘米，底径 20.6 厘米，重 5.86
千克

1965 年平坝县马场熊家坡平 M56 出土

泥质灰陶，通体涂褐色。直口稍外侈，圆唇，肩上置桥形系，
四横二竖，椭圆腹，底微上凹，过系有一周凹弦纹。

釉陶罐

Glazed pottery *guan* jar

Tang Dynasty

唐

高 35.8 厘米，口径 15 厘米，底径 9.6 厘米，重 2698.9 克

1966 年平坝县马场大松山平 M59 出土

泥质灰陶，通体施黑釉，并作漩涡纹斑点。器形腹大底小，直口，口沿外侈，圆鼓腹，腹下收缩较长，小平底。

瓷坛
Porcelain *tan* **jar**
Tang Dynasty

唐
高 14.8 厘米，内口径 8.8 厘米，底径 10.5 厘米，重
907.4 克
1966 年平坝县马场熊家坡出土

施黄绿色开片釉，釉部分脱落。直口，内口微圆唇，外口
唇尖，外侈，肩上置桥形系，椭圆腹，平底，底边稍向外敞。

陶釜

Pottery *fu* caldron

Song Dynasty

宋

高 15 厘米，口径 16 厘米，重 720.4 克

1966 年平坝县马场坝脚平 M65 出土

夹粗砂灰陶，器内外呈深灰色。敞口内敛，方唇，椭圆腹，圜底，外壁通体饰不规则的方格纹，外口沿布纹明显。

陶釜

Pottery *fu* caldron

Song Dynasty

宋

高 17.2 厘米，口径 18.6 厘米，重 931.4 克

1966 年平坝县马场坝脚平 M60 出土

夹砂灰陶。口沿破缺已修复，口沿微内敛，敞口，方唇，椭圆腹，圜底，通体饰菱形纹。

陶釜

Pottery *fu* caldron

Song Dynasty

宋

高 17 厘米，口径 19.8 厘米，重 1072.9 克

1966 年平坝县马场坝脚平 M63 出土

夹砂灰陶。敞口，口沿微内敛，方唇，椭圆腹下垂，圜底，
外壁饰方格纹。

釉陶罐
Glazed pottery *guan* jar
Song Dynasty

宋

高 18.6 厘米，口径 10 厘米，底径 9 厘米，重 1170.5 克

1966 年平坝县马场坝脚平 M62 出土

黄色胎，器内外施褐釉，因轮制痕明显，故釉深浅不同，形成有规律的黄、绿、褐色相间的弦纹轴，近底处无釉。侈口，唇沿外卷，矮领，肩上置桥形系，系座为三瓣花，连接一圆柱，柱弯成半圆形的系，圆鼓腹，小平底，系中间有一周刻在胎上的双线曲波纹。

釉陶罐

Glazed pottery *guan* jar

Song Dynasty

宋
高 12.7 厘米，口径 14.4 厘米，足径 8 厘米，重 525 克
1966 年平坝县马场坝脚平 M60 出土

器内外施深褐色冰裂纹釉，现大部分脱落。基本完整，口
至腹部有一条裂纹，侈口，肩置桥形系，扁圆鼓腹，圈足。

陶釜

Pottery *fu* caldron

Ming Dynasty

明

高 14.8 厘米，口径 16 厘米，重 880.9 克

1966 年平坝县马场坝脚平 M63 出土

陶质较粗，通体涂灰色。口沿残缺部分，并有两条裂缝，腹底有裂纹，敞口，方唇，椭圆腹下垂，圜底，外壁印不规则方格纹，口沿外印纹较浅。

釉陶罐

Glazed pottery *guan* jar

Ming Dynasty

明
高 14 厘米，口径 9.8 厘米，重 415.6 克
1966 年平坝县马场坝脚平 M63 出土

器内壁大部分施薄釉，外壁施黑釉，露灰白色胎，胎釉相接处不齐。直口，圆唇外卷，高领，圆鼓腹，平底，底边沿向外撇。

青花瓷瓶

Blue-and-white porcelain *ping* bottle

Qing Dynasty

清

高 28.5 厘米，外口径 8.06 厘米，内口径 7.35 厘米，最大腹径 13.8 厘米，底径 8.5 厘米

2014 年马场镇出土

圆唇，长颈，鼓腹，腹最大径偏上，平底，颈部有青花"福"字，腹部饰折枝花卉纹。

伍

金银器

银手圈

Silver bracelet

Han Dynasty

汉

直径 6.9 厘米，重 23.6 克

1959 年清镇县芦狄乡新新桥清 M56 出土

圆环不开口，圈梗扁形，断口呈口形。

银珠

Silver beads

Han Dynasty

汉

重 1.2 克

1959 年清镇县芦狄乡新新桥清 M56 出土

圆珠，有穿孔处为平面，孔非直穿，为鼻形。应为帽珠。

银戒指

Silver rings

Han Dynasty

汉

直径 1.8 厘米，重 2.4 克

1965 年平坝县马场熊家坡平 M56 出土

圆环不开口，圈梗宽平，外刻竖道纹。

金钗

Golden *chai* hairpin

Wei, Jin, Northern and Southern Dynasties

魏晋南北朝

横宽 6.1 厘米，足长 7.4 厘米，重 10 克

1957 年平坝县夏云尹关平 M10 出土

金色橙黄如新，顶部弯曲成三弯，大弯扁平，两足为细金条，插入发内。

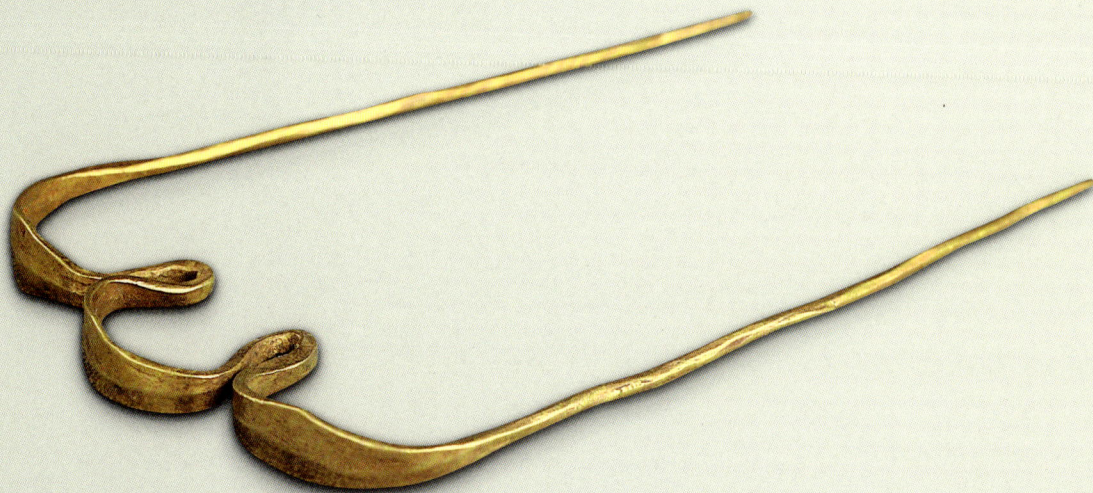

金钗

Golden *chai* hairpin

Wei, Jin, Northern and Southern Dynasties

魏晋南北朝
横宽 6.8 厘米，足长 7.9 厘米，重 9.3 克
1957 年平坝县夏云尹关平 M10 出土

金色橙黄如新，顶部弯曲成三弯，大弯扁平，两足为细金条，
插入发内，一足尖弯曲成钩。

金钗

Golden *chai* hairpins

Wei, Jin, Northern and Southern Dynasties

魏晋南北朝

上：横宽 6.6 厘米，足长 9.3 厘米，重 19.6 克；下：横宽
6.2 厘米，足长 10 厘米，重 23.2 克

1957 年平坝县夏云尹关平 M9 出土

金色橙黄如新，顶部弯曲成三弯，大弯扁平，小弯圆，两
脚下端尖锥形。

金钗

Golden *chai* hairpin

Wei, Jin, Northern and Southern Dynasties

魏晋南北朝

横宽 7.1 厘米，足长 9 厘米，重 43 克

1965 年平坝县马场万人坟平 M34 出土

顶部弯曲成三弯，大弯扁平，小弯圆，两脚下端尖锥形。

金钗

Golden *chai* hairpins

Wei, Jin, Northern and Southern Dynasties

魏晋南北朝

横宽 6.4 ～ 7.2 厘米，足长 7.1 ～ 7.3 厘米，重 35.5 克

1965 年平坝县马场万人坟平 M37 出土

三只，其中两只顶部为三弯形，一只为两弯形，均为两脚。

金钗

Golden *chai* hairpin

Wei, Jin, Northern and Southern Dynasties

魏晋南北朝

横宽 5 厘米，足长 6.8 厘米，重 14.9 克

1957 年平坝县夏云尹关平 M9 出土

金色橙黄如新，顶部弯曲成两弯，两脚下端尖锥形。

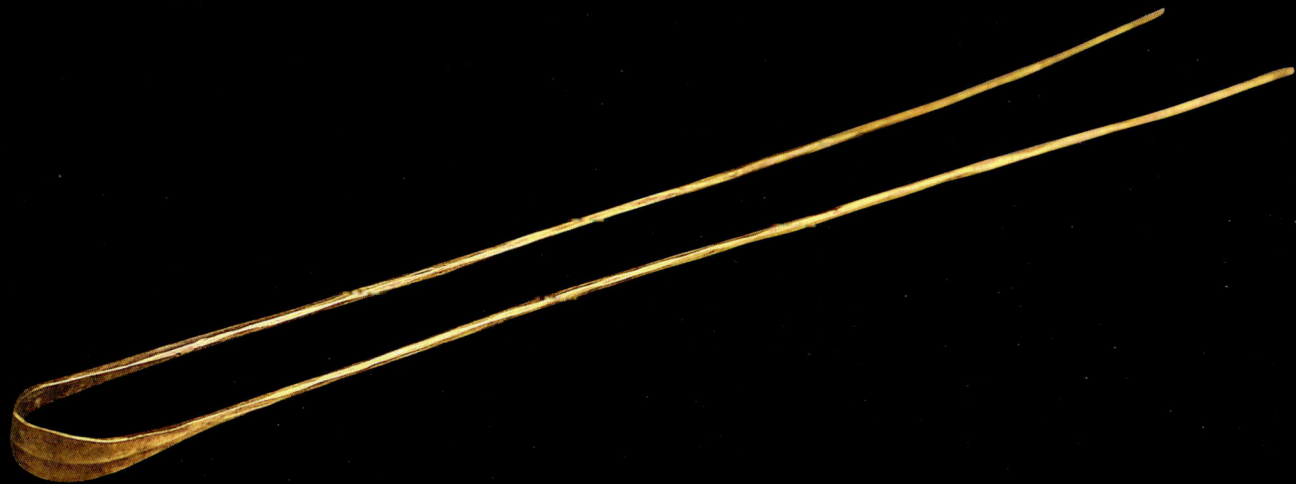

金钗

Golden *chai* hairpin

Wei, Jin, Northern and Southern Dynasties

魏晋南北朝

长 17.5 厘米，重 9.5 克

1957 年平坝县夏云尹关平 M9 出土

金色橙黄如新，两脚特长，顶部扁平成符片，正面有一条棱。

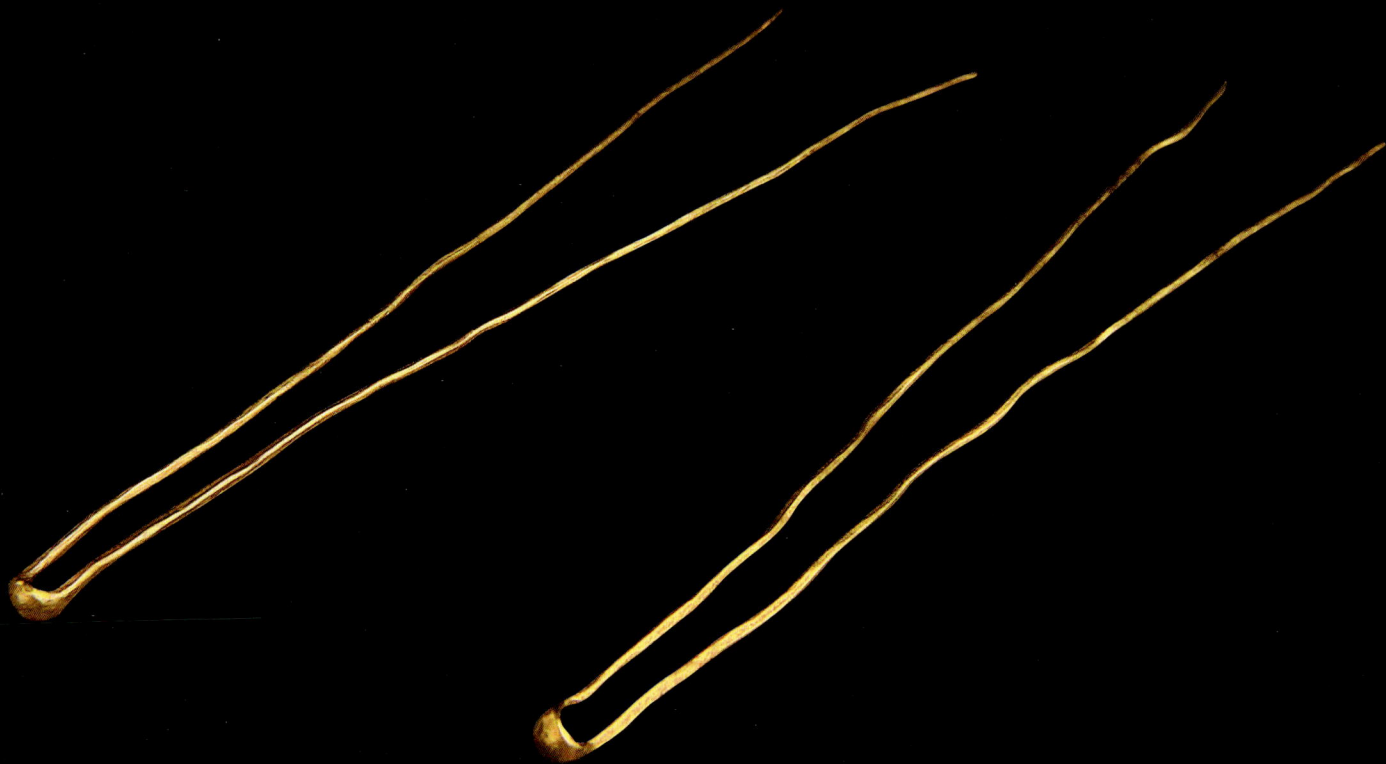

金钗

Golden *chai* hairpins

Wei, Jin, Northern and Southern Dynasties

魏晋南北朝

左：顶径 0.7 厘米，长 21 厘米，重 40.2 克；

右：顶径 0.7 厘米，长 21.3 厘米，重 40.2 克

1965 年平坝县马场万人坟平 M37 出土

长条形，有两长脚，上端为圆形小顶。

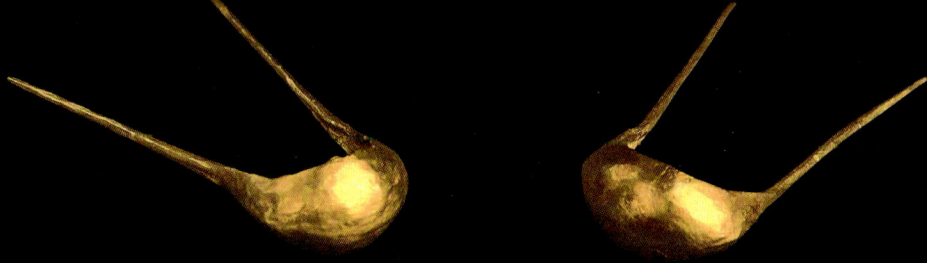

金钗

Golden *chai* hairpins

Wei, Jin, Northern and Southern Dynasties

魏晋南北朝

长 5.2 厘米，宽 2.1 厘米，重 8.9 克

1965 年平坝县马场熊家坡平 M45 出土

色泽橙黄如新，顶部弯拱为双层半圆形帽状，两侧延伸两脚。

金簪

Golden *zan* hairpin

Wei, Jin, Northern and Southern Dynasties

魏晋南北朝

长 19.3 厘米，重 27.4 克

1965 年平坝县马场大松山平 M55 出土

长条形，上端似一莲蓬形，下端吸缩为圆尖针，通体为实
体全条锻打痕。

金花发针

Fazhen hairpin with golden flower

Wei, Jin, Northern and Southern Dynasties

魏晋南北朝

长 17.5 厘米，重 10.8 克

1965 年平坝县马场万人坟平 M37 出土

微残，银针断为数节，长条形银针，上端有金花四瓣，分
别在银针两侧。

金花发针

Fazhen hairpin with golden flower

Wei, Jin, Northern and Southern Dynasties

魏晋南北朝

长 18.2 厘米，重 10.2 克

1965 年平坝县马场万人坟平 M34 出土

微残，针尖断缺，金花有压损已在针杆不能固定，金花四瓣，长似叶状，发针一端作挖耳，针系银质。

金戒指

Golden ring

Wei, Jin, Northern and Southern Dynasties

魏晋南北朝

直径 1.8 厘米，边宽 0.4 厘米，重 6.1 克

1965 年平坝县马场熊家坡平 M46 出土

圆箍不和，上下平口，内壁平，外壁略凸光滑，环体较宽。

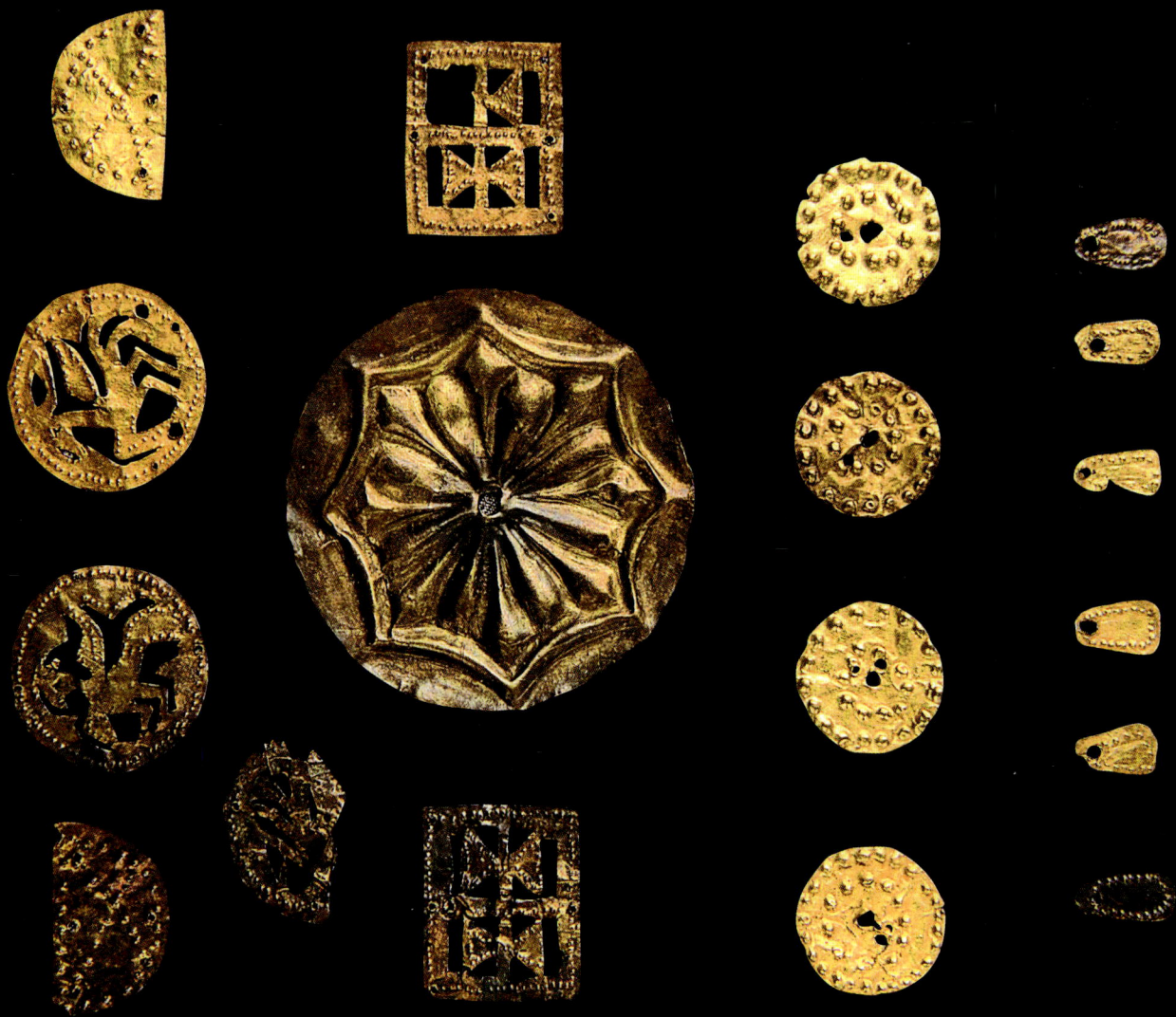

金花片

Golden sheets with various design

Wei, Jin, Northern and Southern Dynasties

魏晋南北朝

最大直径5.4厘米，方2.6×2.1厘米，圆径1.9～2.7厘米，半圆径2.5厘米，重13.1克

1965年平坝县马场万人坟平M34出土

共18件，一片残半，其余完整。金片形状分六类，一类圆形压印菊花瓣纹，一片，色呈黄黑；第二类，圆形錾一鸡纹，三片（残一片）；第三类长方形中分四格錾三角形图案，两片；第四类，圆片，钉满小乳钉纹，共四片；第五类，半圆片，两片；第六类椭圆形小片。

金花片

Golden sheets with various design

Wei, Jin, Northern and Southern Dynasties

魏晋南北朝

大圆径 3 厘米，锥形长 1.8 厘米，小圆径 2.4 厘米，半圆径 2.5 厘米

1965 年平坝县马场万人坟平 M37 出土

共 20 件，圆形金片 12 片，半圆形 2 片，锥形 5 片，金丝扭成的小环形 1 件。

表面均有小孔，一圆形和一半圆形金片上有小孔组成蛙形。

金花片
Flower-shaped golden sheet
Wei, Jin, Northern and Southern Dynasties

魏晋南北朝
直径 5.3 厘米，重 5.4 克
1965 年平坝县马场熊家坡平 M41 出土

圆形，正中一孔，菊花纹，原有一铜泡钉
穿金片孔中。

金花片
Flower-shaped golden sheet
Wei, Jin, Northern and Southern Dynasties

魏晋南北朝
直径 5.1 ～ 5.2 厘米，重 4.8 克
1965 年平坝县马场熊家坡平 M44 出土

圆薄片中间一孔穿钉形银插针一枚，金片
压印菊花纹，外圈压八连弧纹。

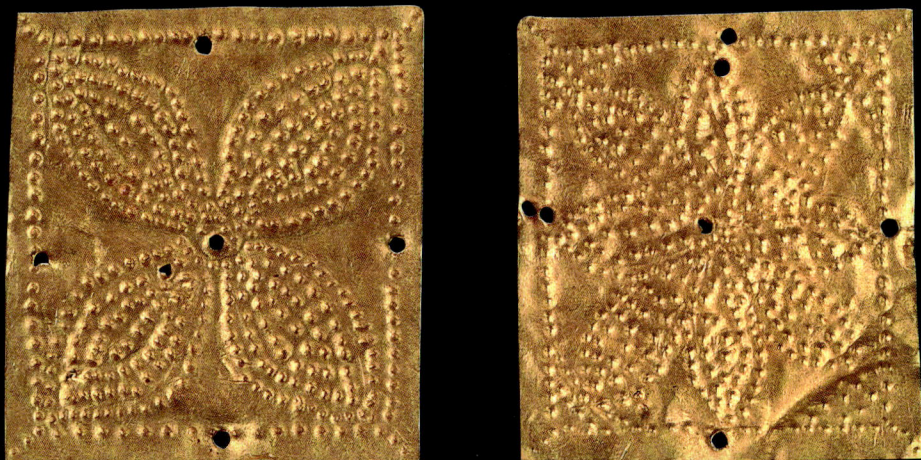

金花片

Golden sheets with flower pattern

Wei, Jin, Northern and Southern Dynasties

魏晋南北朝

长 3 厘米，宽 2.9 厘米，重 3.3 克

1965 年平坝县马场万人坟平 M37 出土

2 件。方形，中间及四周均有小孔，一件用小孔做成四瓣花纹，一件用小孔做成八瓣花纹。

金珠

Golden beads

Wei, Jin, Northern and Southern Dynasties

魏晋南北朝

直径 1.3 厘米，重 7.9 克

1965 年平坝县马场万人坟平 M37 出土

近珠形，腰有一道合缝，上下端各有六个凸出的小圆点，似一朵梅花。

银钗

Silver *chai* hairpin

Wei, Jin, Northern and Southern Dynasties

魏晋南北朝

长 10 厘米，宽 9.6 厘米，重 22.7 克

1957 年平坝县夏云尹关平 M9 出土

顶部扁平，弯成两弯，下部两脚，一脚尖弯曲向上勾。

银钗

Silver *chai* hairpins

Wei, Jin, Northern and Southern Dynasties

魏晋南北朝

长 10.7 厘米，重 33.7 克

1965 年平坝县马场万人坟平 M34 出土

顶部弯曲成三弯，大弯平扁，有两脚，下端尖。

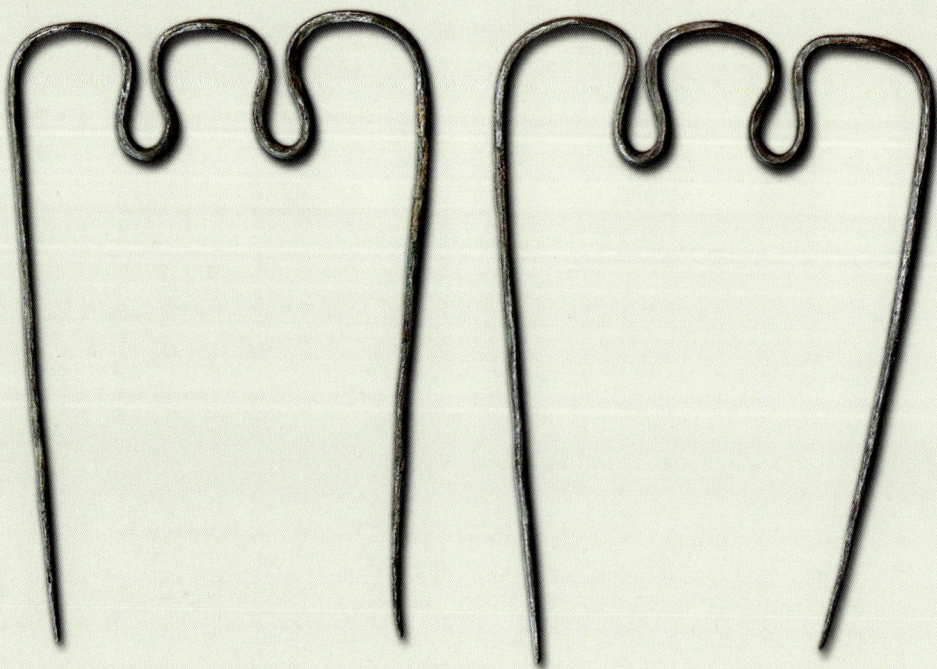

银钗

Silver *chai* hairpin

Wei, Jin, Northern and Southern Dynasties

魏晋南北朝

长 14 厘米，宽 6 厘米，重 84.3 克

1965 年平坝县马场万人坟平 M37 出土

弧形盖顶，顶上有空心的圆乳点，下端两长脚。

银发针

Silver *fazhen* hairpin

Wei, Jin, Northern and Southern Dynasties

魏晋南北朝

长 20.2 厘米，重 19.6 克

1957 年平坝县夏云尹关平 M9 出土

双股长脚，顶上扭成三瓣形，脚残断。

银戒指

Sliver ring
Wei, Jin, Northern and Southern Dynasties

魏晋南北朝
直径 2 厘米，重 5.6 克
1959 年清镇县大冈牧马场清 M110 出土

银条绕成三环，不开口。

银挖耳插针

Silver needle with earpick
Wei, Jin, Northern and Southern Dynasties

魏晋南北朝
长 17.5 厘米，重 6.7 克
1965 年平坝县马场万人坟平 M37 出土

已残断，长条圆柱形，下端有一小勺。

银条脱

Silver *tiaotuo* accessory

Wei, Jin, Northern and Southern Dynasties

魏晋南北朝

直径 6.3 厘米，重 50 克

1965 年平坝县马场熊家坡平 M42 出土

圈作三环，开口处以扭丝缠绕，宽环处作圈点纹，两端作竖道纹。

银顶针

Silver *dingzhen* thimble
Wei, Jin, Northern and Southern Dynasties

魏晋南北朝
直径 2 厘米，宽 1.2 厘米，重 7.6 克
1965 年平坝县马场万人坟平 M37 出土

深灰色，两端卷边，面有四行圆点凹纹。

银铃

Silver *ling* bells
Wei, Jin, Northern and Southern Dynasties

魏晋南北朝
直径 1.5 厘米，重 11.3 克
1965 年平坝县马场万人坟平 M37 出土

灰色，铃为球形，上端有一环形系，下端有一字形小口，
现无铃舌。

金戒指

Golden rings

Tang Dynasty

唐

直径 1.8 厘米，重 7.2 克

1965 年平坝县马场熊家坡平 M56 出土

圆环不开口，圈梗宽平，外刻竖道纹。

银条脱

Silver *tiaotuo* accessory

Tang Dynasty

唐

直径 6.8 厘米，重 111.9 克

1965 年平坝县马场熊家坡平 M47 出土

微残，两端缠绕处断杇，长条圆梗，两端
略细，绕成圆环五层，口两端细丝各缠绕
在第二环上，可缩可张，旋放似弹簧状。

铜銷

Bronze *juan* vessel
Western Han Dynasty

西汉
高 10 厘米，口径 20 厘米，底径 10 厘米，重 723.2 克
1957 年平坝县夏云尹关平 M70 出土

折口，圆唇，深腹，小平底。

双鱼纹铜洗

Bronze *xi* basin with fish pattern

Eastern Han Dynasty

东汉

高 7 厘米，口径 32.5 厘米，底径 18.4 厘米，重 1952.2 克

1959 年平坝县夏云尹关平 M16 出土

残，口破裂三处，部分弯形。敞口，折沿，浅直腹，腹外壁有一对铺首衔环耳，外底呈四条旋棱之假圈足，内底心下凹处有双鱼吐钱花纹，为模铸。

三足铜水注
Three-legged bronze *shuizhu* vessel
Eastern Han Dynasty

东汉
高 6.2 厘米, 口径 1.9 厘米, 最大腹径 6.8 厘米, 重 240.1 克
1959 年平坝县夏云尹关平 M16 出土

圆形小口, 短颈, 圆鼓腹, 圜底, 底部有三只蹄足, 腹部
等距附三只对称的管形装饰。

铜洗

Bronze *xi* basin

Han Dynasty

汉

高 7.4 厘米，口径 20.8 厘米，重 301.1 克

1959 年清镇县芦荻新新桥清 M74 出土

微残，底沿有一小洞。直口，口沿外折，深腹，圈底。

铜釜

Bronze *fu* caldron

Han Dynasty

汉

高 8.6 厘米，口径 13.6 厘米，足径 5.8 厘米，重 252.2 克

1958 年清镇县芦荻新新桥清 M56 出土

微残，口沿、一耳经石膏修补。敞口，宽口沿内折，两耳直
立于口沿，作辫索纹圈耳，耳上又各立一兽或鸟，圆鼓腹，
矮圈足，圈内有四乳足。

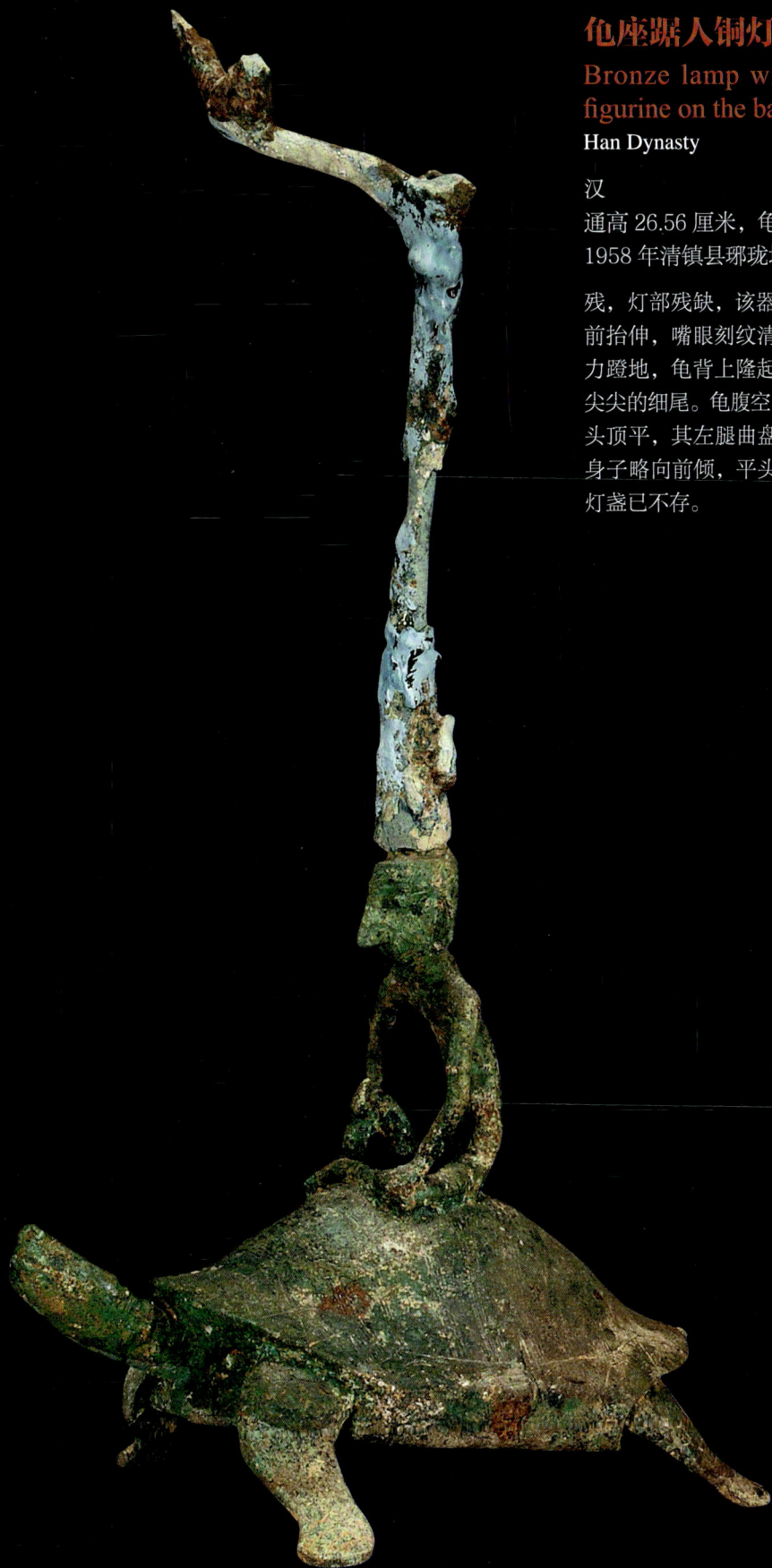

龟座踞人铜灯

Bronze lamp with turtle-shaped base (and a figurine on the back of the turtle)

Han Dynasty

汉

通高 26.56 厘米，龟长 17 厘米，重 808.1 克

1958 年清镇县琊珑坝清 M15 出土

残，灯部残缺，该器为复合器。底部乌龟作爬行状，头向前抬伸，嘴眼刻纹清晰，两前足呈八字形外撇，两后足用力蹬地，龟背上隆起的厚甲将整个龟身罩住，甲后露出一尖尖的细尾。龟腹空，龟背上坐一男子，鹰鼻深目，大耳，头顶平，其左腿曲盘，右腿曲蹲，双手扶于膝盖上，整个身子略向前倾，平头顶立一长柱形灯杆，柱顶分枝已残，灯盏已不存。

铜马铃
Bronze horse bell
Han Dynasty

汉
高 5.2 厘米，宽 5.9 厘米，重 31.8 克
1959 年平坝县夏云尹关平 M22 出土

微残，两面均有破洞。顶部左右伸出两孔为穿绳索，绳中
吊一舌，挂于马脖，即会叮当作响。

铜环
Bronze ring
Han Dynasty

汉
外径 2.3 厘米，内径 1.7 厘米，高 0.35 厘米
2014 年平坝县夏云尹关、母猪龙潭汉墓群出土

圆形，断面略呈方形。

铜釜

Bronze *fu* caldron

Wei, Jin, Northern and Southern Dynasties

魏晋南北朝

高 17.9 厘米，口径 20 厘米，最大腹径 21.5 厘米，重 1244.2 克

1957 年平坝县夏云尹关平 M70 出土

残，敞口，圆扁腹，腹上部有一对片状孔耳，圜底，腹部有两周凸弦纹。

铜釜

Bronze *fu* caldron

Wei, Jin, Northern and Southern Dynasties

魏晋南北朝

高 10 厘米，口径 20 厘米，最大腹径 17.8 厘米

1957 年平坝县夏云尹关平 M9 出土

敞口，口沿内仰，圆鼓腹，平底，底上凸，上腹有三周凸弦纹，
纹下有穿耳一对。

铜釜

Bronze *fu* caldron
Wei, Jin, Northern and Southern Dynasties

魏晋南北朝
高 9.6 厘米，口径 10.5 厘米，最大腹径 11.8 厘米，重
403.7 克
1965 年平坝县马场万人坟平 M36 出土

微残，底部有二破洞。敞口，唇尖微敛，颈下两环耳对称，
圆腹，腹上起一道棱。

铜釜

Bronze *fu* caldron

Wei, Jin, Northern and Southern Dynasties

魏晋南北朝

高 15.6 厘米，口径 22.5 厘米，最大腹径 18.9 厘米，重 841.8 克

1965 年平坝县马场熊家坡平 M54 出土

侈口，尖唇内卷，颈下两环耳对称，圆鼓腹，圜底，口沿有一周凸弦纹，腹部有三周凸弦纹，因锈蚀，均已模糊不清。

带柄铜釜

Bronze *fu* caldron with handle
Wei, Jin, Northern and Southern Dynasties

魏晋南北朝
高 11.5 厘米，口径 12.7 厘米，柄长 27.5 厘米，重 959.7 克
1957 年平坝县夏云尹关平 M9 出土

微残，铁柄锈残。敞口，口沿外翻，束颈，圆鼓腹，上腹环
耳仅存一只，圜底。铁柄为开口箍形，箍于釜颈把长，便于
炊事。

带柄铜釜

Bronze *fu* caldron with handle
Wei, Jin, Northern and Southern Dynasties

魏晋南北朝
高 10 厘米，口径 13.2 厘米，柄长 20.8 厘米，重 756.2 克
1965 年平坝县马场万人坟平 M34 出土

釜完整，铁把已残断脱落。敞口，圜底，腹肩上两环耳对称。
铁柄圆箍通过环耳，柄略弯长，烹饪时避免烫手，出土时釜
内尚有兽骨两块。

带柄铜釜

Bronze *fu* caldron with handle

Wei, Jin, Northern and Southern Dynasties

魏晋南北朝

高 9.8 厘米，口径 11 厘米，柄长 33 厘米，重 864.4 克

1965 年平坝县马场万人坟平 M42 出土

微残，侈口，尖唇内卷，圆腹，颈下两环耳对称，圜底，腹部有两周凸弦纹。带柄铁箍穿过两耳，以便炊用。

铜洗

Bronze *xi* basin

Wei, Jin, Northern and Southern Dynasties

魏晋南北朝

高 9 厘米，口径 20.7 厘米，重 1194.2 克

1965 年平坝县马场万人坟平 M34 出土

敞口，口沿下凸起一棱，平底，蹄足，底内有双鱼纹，腹上有五周凸弦纹。

铜洗

Bronze *xi* basin
Wei, Jin, Northern and Southern Dynasties

魏晋南北朝
高 10.3 厘米，口径 28.8 厘米，重 1736.4 克
1957 年平坝县夏云尹关平 M7 出土

口沿外折，腹微鼓，腹部有耳穿各一对，耳上原可能有环，
现不存，三足象鼻形，腹部有四周凸弦纹。

铜托杯

Bronze cup with saucer

Wei, Jin, Northern and Southern Dynasties

魏晋南北朝

通高 9.5 厘米；杯高 7.9 厘米，口径 7.8 厘米，足径 2.8 厘米；托盘直径
13.5 厘米，足径 5.9 厘米；重 436.2 克

1957 年平坝县夏云尹关平 M7 出土

微残，珠纽断，接补。托杯上有杯盖，下有托盘，精致美观。杯直口，圆腹，盖
上凸，珠顶形纽，杯外口腹上有三、四、六周复线刻划弦纹，盖上也有单、双线
四周弦纹。托盘平，盘口沿上翻，中心有承杯足之圈，底有圈足。

铜托杯

Bronze cup with saucer

Wei, Jin, Northern and Southern Dynasties

魏晋南北朝

通高 12.6 厘米，杯口径 9.6 厘米，盘径 16.8 厘米，重 473.4 克

1965 年平坝县马场万人坟平 M36 出土

由杯盖、杯和托盘三部分组合而成，造形简洁。杯盖扣在杯口，直径与杯口径相同，盖顶正中有尖柱状纽，盖面两圆弧圈。杯敞口，口沿外侈，下腹内折，立于一青铜短柱上，铜柱与托盘相接。托盘敞口、较浅，腹部曲折，高圈足。

铜镳斗

Bronze *jiaodou* vessel

Wei, Jin, Northern and Southern Dynasties

魏晋南北朝

高 10.8 厘米，口径 13.8 厘米，柄长 24.5 厘米，重
968.6 克

1957 年平坝县夏云尹关平 M9 出土

口沿外仰折，有流，椭圆腹，圜底，三足呈马蹄状，足瘦长，
长柄。

铜镟斗

Bronze *jiaodou* vessel

Wei, Jin, Northern and Southern Dynasties

魏晋南北朝

高 10.6 厘米，口径 13.5 厘米，重 784.2 克

1965 年平坝县马场万人坟平 M34 出土

口唇外折，有流，长把，腹壁直，腹下三兽足。

铁柄铜鐎斗

Bronze *jiaodou* vessel with iron handle

Wei, Jin, Northern and Southern Dynasties

魏晋南北朝

高 9.3 厘米，口径 14.1 厘米，底径 10.8 厘米，柄长
21.5 厘米，重 761.8 克

1965 年平坝县马场万人坟平 M37 出土

微残，铁柄断，铜鐎斗流残。敞口，有流，圜底，三直足，
流右侧有一带铁圈之长柄。

铜镜

Bronze mirror

Wei, Jin, Northern and Southern Dynasties

魏晋南北朝

直径 12.5 厘米，厚 0.5 厘米，重 301.6 克

1965 年平坝县马场万人坟平 M34 出土

黑漆发亮，略带铜斑，镜上纹饰分两圈，外圈八连弧纹，
内圈四瓣草叶纹，叶间相隔篆书阳文"长宜子孙"四字。

铜镜

Bronze mirror

Wei, Jin, Northern and Southern Dynasties

魏晋南北朝
直径 15 厘米，重 551.5 克
1965 年平坝县马场万人坟平 M37 出土

半球形纽，纽外一周为四神四兽纹，再外圈为铭文，铭文
外为锯齿纹，再外圈为凤鸟纹，最外一圈为变形夔纹。

带链铜夹

Bronze clip with chain

Wei, Jin, Northern and Southern Dynasties

魏晋南北朝
通长 18 厘米，夹长 6 厘米，重 9.6 克
1965 年平坝县马场熊家坡平 M45 出土

铜夹由一块长条形铜片制成，中间窄，两端宽，从正中弯
成环孔之后合并，两端稍弯曲使之成夹，夹之中部以银丝
绾住，夹下系一根由银丝制成之链。

铜簪

Bronze *zan* hairpins

Wei, Jin, Northern and Southern Dynasties

魏晋南北朝

长 24.8 厘米，重 69.4 克

1965 年平坝县马场熊家坡平 M50 出土

残，下部两长脚相并，上部为戟形饰，刻有六勾纹。

鎏金铜钗
Gilding bronze *chai* hairpin
Wei, Jin, Northern and Southern Dynasties

魏晋南北朝
长 11.7 厘米，宽 5.3 厘米，重 14.7 克
1965 年平坝县马场熊家坡平 M42 出土

微残，顶边沿有破洞一处。表面鎏金原被铜锈遮盖，去锈
金光发亮，顶部为双层弧形，外沿合拢，内沿双层张开，
并作双弧形，下为两脚。

铜手圈
Bronze bracelets
Wei, Jin, Northern and Southern Dynasties

魏晋南北朝
直径 6.4 厘米，重 28.8 克
1965 年平坝县马场熊家坡平 M41 出土

圈面为弧形。

铜条脱

Bronze *tiaotuo* accessory

Wei, Jin, Northern and Southern Dynasties

魏晋南北朝

长 16.2 厘米，直径 6.6 厘米，条径 0.3
厘米，重 68.9 克

1965 年平坝县马场熊家坡平 M46 出土

铜质鎏金，现全已剥落，仅在阳光下还隐
约可见，铜圆条绕环七圈，两端铜条较细，
各以一端绕缠在第二圈上，并可缩放。

铜戒指

Bronze rings

Wei, Jin, Northern and Southern Dynasties

魏晋南北朝

直径 2 厘米，重 6.2 克

1965 年平坝县马场熊家坡平 M48 出土

环状不开口，圈梗内壁略凹、外壁略凸，外壁饰竖线纹。

铁鼎

Iron *ding* vessel

Wei, Jin, Northern and Southern Dynasties

魏晋南北朝
高 20.5 厘米，口径 26.5 厘米，重 3.02 千克
1959 年清镇县芦荻哨清芦 M35 出土

残，锈蚀严重。敞口，圜底，下有三足，一耳残。

铁剪刀

Iron scissor

Wei, Jin, Northern and Southern Dynasties

魏晋南北朝

长 21 厘米，重 303.2 克

1959 年清镇县大冈马场清 M110 出土

一根铁棒，两端煅打成刀片，然后下弯成 8 字交叉即成，
无铆类固定之物。

铁棺钉

Iron coffin nails

Wei, Jin, Northern and Southern Dynasties

魏晋南北朝

最长 14 厘米，重 71.2 克

1965 年平坝县马场万人坟平 M37 出土

分为三种类型，一种为方形钉帽，一种为圆形钉帽，一种
为折钩形钉帽。

铁矛

Iron spear

Song Dynasty

宋

长 30.2 厘米，重 217.4 克

1959 年清镇县芦荻哨清 M65 出土

双面刃，尖锋，鸭嘴銎，銎上一箍棱。实用武器。

铜钗

Bronze *chai* hairpin

Song Dynasty

宋

长 35 厘米，宽 0.8 厘米，重 72.4 克

1966 年平坝县马场熊家坡平 M62 出土

长条形，两脚，顶部弯曲，距顶部 1 厘米处用细铜丝加固。

铜钗

Bronze *chai* hairpin

Song Dynasty

宋

长 32.7 厘米，重 80.6 克

1966 年平坝县马场坝脚平 M64 出土

圆条形，从中段弯曲处并以铜丝缠绕加固。

铜戒指
Bronze rings
Song Dynasty

宋
直径 2 厘米，边宽 0.4 厘米，重 4.8 克
1966 年平坝县马场坝脚平 M65 出土

圆环开口，宽边，正面圆形上刻钱币纹。

铜手圈
Bronze bracelets
Tang Dynasty

唐
直径 7.4 厘米，边宽 0.6 厘米，重 80.2 克
1965 年平坝县马场熊家坡平 M47 出土

圆环不开口，圈外作锯齿纹。

铜镜

Bronze mirror

Tang Dynasty

唐

直径 10.1 厘米，厚 1.1 厘米，重 347.3 克

1965 年平坝县马场熊家坡平 M54 出土

通体漆黑发亮，圆纽，边缘及内区凸起两周，边缘凸起一周高于内区一周。

铁棺钉
Iron coffin nails

Tang Dynasty

唐

长分别为 12.2、16.2、19.8 厘米，重 108.4 克

1965 年平坝县马场镇熊家坡平 M40 出土

长条形，上端向一侧折成钉帽，断面方形。

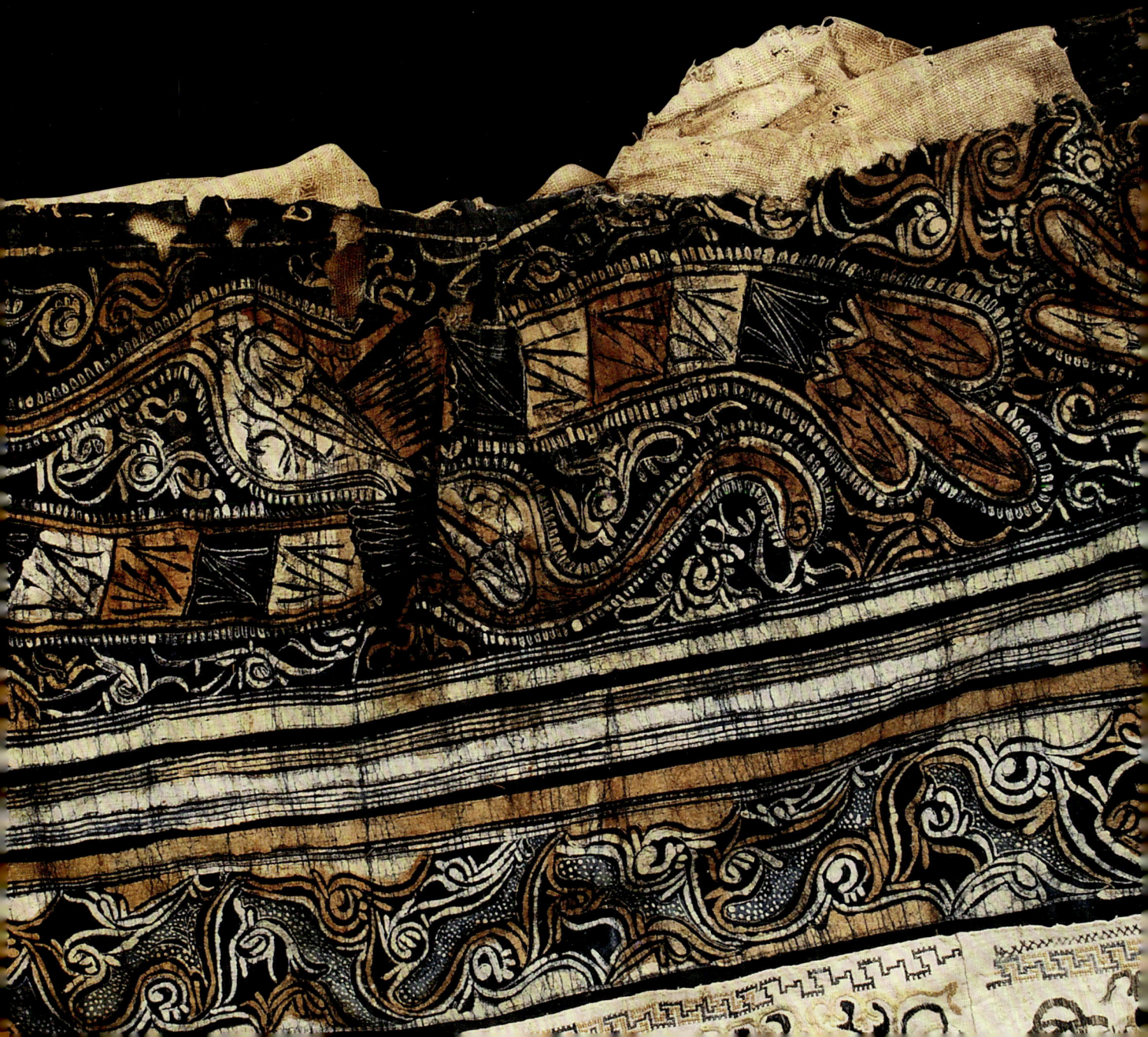

琉璃耳珰

Colored glaze *erdang* eardrop

Han Dynasty

汉

高 1.6 厘米，两端直径 1.8、1.1 厘米，最小腹径 0.8 厘米，孔径 0.17 厘米

2014 年平坝县夏云尹关、母猪龙潭汉墓群出土

淡蓝色，半透明，横剖面为圆形，纵剖面略呈亚腰形，中间略呈圆柱体，向两端逐渐宽出柱径，柱中心有一圆孔贯通，孔两端略内凹。

琥珀狮坠
Lion-shaped amber accessories
Han Dynasty

汉
高 1.2 ~ 1.3 厘米，长 1.7 ~ 1.9 厘米，重 3.4 克
1959 年清镇县芦狄新新桥清 M56 出土

一枚茶褐色，一枚棕色，外观形态基本完整，其中一只底部有裂纹，狮形作蹲伏状，腹下有一穿孔。

玻璃羊坠
Sheep-shaped glass accessory
Han Dynasty

汉
高 1.3 厘米，长 1.6 厘米，重 3.3 克
1959 年清镇县芦狄新新桥清 M56 出土

绿色透明，一只耳残，足磕伤，左侧有裂口，羊作蹲伏状。

串珠

A string of beads

Wei, Jin, Northern and Southern Dynasties

魏晋南北朝

长 35 厘米，重 24.4 克

1957 年平坝县夏云尹关平 M9 出土

共 213 粒，圆形小珠，如绿豆大小，有红、黄、黑、绿色等，
其中有三颗较大的，三颗次大的，另有四个银簧管。

串珠

A string of beads

Wei, Jin, Northern and Southern Dynasties

魏晋南北朝
总长 33.5 厘米
2014 年马场镇杨家桥遗址 M1 出土

有红、蓝、黄、绿、黑几种颜色珠子，材
质有琉璃、石、金属等，大小、长短不一，
形状有圆形、柱形、管形。

串珠

A string of beads

Wei, Jin, Northern and Southern Dynasties

魏晋南北朝
长 15.7 厘米，重 78.2 克
1965 年平坝县马场熊家坡平 M46 出土

圆球状珠居多，另有菱形玛瑙珠、琥珀坠。

串珠

A string of beads

Wei, Jin, Northern and Southern Dynasties

魏晋南北朝
长 16 厘米，重 50.9 克
1959 年清镇县大冈牧马场清 M105 出土

36 颗，蓝色居多，另有绿色、玛瑙红、蜜蜡红、黄色等。

串珠

A string of beads

Wei, Jin, Northern and Southern Dynasties

魏晋南北朝
长 21.5 厘米，重 17.5 克
1959 年清镇县大冈牧马场清 M104 出土

绿豆大的多数，有 6 颗稍大如黄豆，蓝色、绿色为多，另
有淡青色，还有非料质的红色蜜蜡珠。

玛瑙珠

Agate bead

Wei, Jin, Northern and Southern Dynasties

魏晋南北朝
直径 1.18 厘米，孔径 0.16 厘米
2014 年马场镇杨家桥遗址 M1 出土

主体呈茶红色，内有白色条带，球形，中间穿孔。

玛瑙珠

Agate bead

Wei, Jin, Northern and Southern Dynasties

魏晋南北朝
直径 1.2 厘米，孔径 0.17 厘米
2014 年马场镇杨家桥遗址 M1 出土

茶红色，内有白色条带，球形，中间穿孔。

玛瑙珠

Agate bead

Wei, Jin, Northern and Southern Dynasties

魏晋南北朝
长 1.54 厘米，直径 1 厘米，孔径 0.12 厘米
2014 年马场镇杨家桥遗址 M1 出土

主体呈淡茶红色，半透明，十二棱橄榄形，中间穿孔。

玛瑙珠

Agate bead

Wei, Jin, Northern and Southern Dynasties

魏晋南北朝
长 1.78 厘米，直径 1.02 厘米，孔径 0.15 厘米
2014 年马场镇杨家桥遗址 M1 出土

主体呈淡茶红色，半透明，内有白色条带，十二棱橄榄形，中间穿孔。

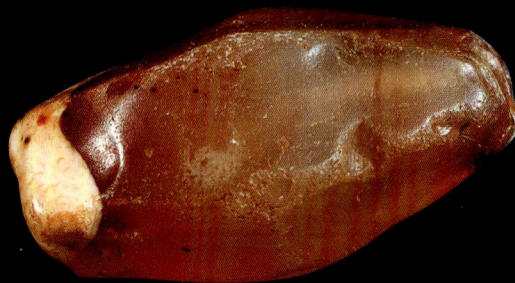

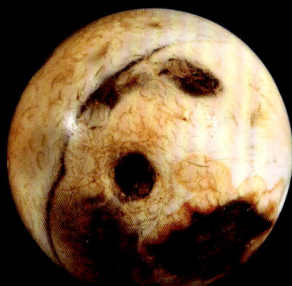

玛瑙珠

Agate bead

Wei, Jin, Northern and Southern Dynasties

魏晋南北朝
直径 1.09 厘米，孔径 0.16 厘米
2014 年马场镇杨家桥遗址 M1 出土

主体乳白色条带较多，球形，中间穿孔。

玛瑙珠

Agate bead

Wei, Jin, Northern and Southern Dynasties

魏晋南北朝
直径 1.34 厘米，孔径 0.16 厘米
2014 年马场镇杨家桥遗址 M1 出土

茶红色，内有褐色条带，球形，中间穿孔。

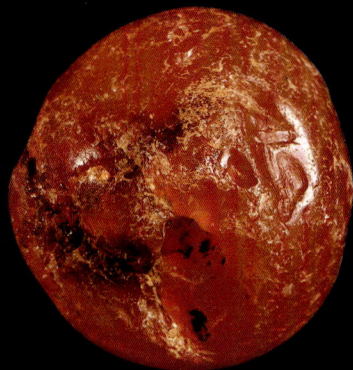

玛瑙珠

Agate bead

Wei, Jin, Northern and Southern Dynasties

魏晋南北朝
长 1.16 厘米，直径 1 厘米，孔径 0.11 厘米
2014 年马场镇杨家桥遗址 M1 出土

主体乳白色条带较多，十二棱短枣核形，中间穿孔。

玛瑙珠

Agate bead

Wei, Jin, Northern and Southern Dynasties

魏晋南北朝
长 1.1 厘米，直径 0.73 厘米，孔径 0.14 厘米
2014 年马场镇杨家桥遗址 M1 出土

主体呈茶红色，内含白色和黑色条带，半透明，八棱橄榄形（枣核形），中间穿孔。

玛瑙珠

Agate bead

Wei, Jin, Northern and Southern Dynasties

魏晋南北朝
直径 1.2 厘米，孔径 0.13 厘米
2014 年马场镇杨家桥遗址 M1 出土

淡茶红色，内有深色条带，球形，中间穿孔。

串珠

A string of beads

Song Dynasty

宋

长 32.9 厘米，重 18.5 克

1965 年平坝县马场坝脚平 M64 出土

由 2 颗黄色圆球形大珠与近 300 颗绿色小珠穿成。

鹭鸟纹彩色蜡染衣裙

Colorful batik clothing with bird pattern

Song Dynasty

宋

衣长72厘米，胸宽55厘米，胸袖宽78厘米，裙长62.5厘米，通横512厘米，重1.64千克

1987年平坝县棺材洞出土

2件套，棉麻纤维质地，微残，有破损。裙腰麻质，衣、裙身棉质，装饰工艺以填彩蜡染为主，兼用挑花和刺绣。裙纹由两个晕带构成，上为主晕，纹样以翔鹭为主，尾羽特长，屈肢昂首展翅，敷彩以黄色为基调，且有深浅之分，并用几何纹饰补空，主晕之下有两组弦纹，下为次晕，纹饰为流云，流云间以米点补空，色彩与主晕相同，渍染的蓝色有浓淡之分，冰纹均为纵向，细腻自然，次晕之下为两晕挑花夹一晕刺绣，挑花为席纹和"万"字纹，刺绣用黄绿二色线绣林木、走兽、人物等，裙边素蓝色。

莲花纹玉饰件
Jade accessory with lotus pattern
Ming Dynasty

明
高 4.82 厘米，底圈高 0.7 厘米，内径 5.7 厘米，壁厚 0.73
厘米，底圈厚 0.37 厘米
2014 年马场镇征集

口略残，圆形，口微敞，器身饰八瓣莲花纹，有黑色条带。

黔中遗珍
贵安新区出土文物精粹

后记

　　1954年羊昌河水利灌溉工程建设时，在羊昌河两岸发现汉墓，从那时算起，在贵安新区境内开展考古工作至今已经有60余年的历史，几次大规模的考古发掘收获巨大，填补了贵州历史的多个空白，出土的一大批精美绝伦的文物，是贵安新区深厚历史文化底蕴的实物鉴证。

　　借中国（贵州）第二届国际民族民间工艺品文化产品博览会之机，举办贵安新区考古成果展和编印宣传画册，有着非常的意义。既是对贵安60年考古工作的梳理和总结，最早在此工作的先生们，如陈默溪先生、熊水富先生、万光云先生已然仙逝，他们的工作成果，如今发挥了应有的社会效益。更是对以后工作的期望。今天，贵安新区的大开发大建设正如火如荼，带来了贵安考古的良机，极大地促进了贵安考古工作的发展，既是机遇，也是挑战，挖掘和保护贵安新区文化遗产，落在了新一代文保人的肩上。配合贵安新区建设的最新考古成果，离不开贵州省文化厅、文物局的大力支持，在省级文物保护专项经费紧张的情况下，还划拨了贵安新区文保专项经费，解决了贵安新区考古专项经费困难的问题。近三年来，贵州省文物考古研究所几乎是倾全所之力，基建和学术相结合，联合中国社会科学院考古研究所、四川大学历史文化学院、成都文物考古研究所等并力推进。事业薪火相传，一代代考古人孜孜不倦、甘于寂寞，奋战在考古一线，新的发现、丰硕的成果正不断面世。

　　本次考古成果展的成功举办和画册的刊印出版，是在贵安新区党工委的高度重视和直接敦促下推进的，提供场地、经费和各方面的工作保障，确保快捷高效。让我们再一次体会到了贵安新区各级领导对文化遗产保护和考古事业的高度重视和关心。之前，秦如培常务副省长就为"贵州考古贵安整理基地（贵州公共考古活动中心）"项目专门签署意见，使得该项目能顺利立项和顺利选址，目前已经完成征地工作。此次展览举办和画册出版，秦如培常务副省长和党工委马长青书记均亲自过问，马长青书记还亲自为作序，这是对我们工作的极大鼓励和鞭策。

　　收入本次展览和画册的文物主要来源于贵州省博物馆、贵州省文物考古研究所、中国社会科学院考古研究所，皆为地下出土文物。贵州省博物馆提供了大量的馆藏文物照片，贵州省博物馆朱良津副馆长、金萍主任、闫冬琼三位同志付出了辛勤劳动。中国社会科学院考古研究所傅宪国主任、傅永旭同志奉献了他们的发掘和研究成果。四川大学历史文化学院张寒冬、徐赛凤、欧阳心怡、齐慧玲、卢林明等同学也参与了部分文物的器物描述撰写工作，贵州画报王飞飞老师负责拍摄了本画册的部分文物，科学出版社柴丽丽同志，在时间紧、任务重的情况下，牺牲了大量休息时间，高质量地完成了本书的编辑工作，保证了画册能按时出版。

　　在此，对以上所有给予我们工作支持的单位、领导及同仁，一并表示感谢。

　　本次展览的策划和画册的撰稿、校对主要由贵州省文物考古研究所周必素所长、张兴龙、杨偲、朱梅同志完成，贵安新区文化艺术博览馆肖霄主任为本书出版付出了辛苦努力。由于时间仓促和撰稿者水平所限，难免有遗漏和错讹之处，敬请指正。

编　者